THE
GREAT WAR ILLUSTRATED
THE HOME FRONT

THE
GREAT WAR ILLUSTRATED
THE HOME FRONT

Deepening Conflict

David Bilton

Pen & Sword
MILITARY

First published in Great Britain in 2016 by
PEN & SWORD MILITARY
an imprint of
Pen & Sword Books Ltd,
47 Church Street, Barnsley,
South Yorkshire.
S70 2AS

ISBN 978 1 47383 3 715

A CIP catalogue record for this book is available
from the British Library

Printed and bound in England by CPI Group (UK) Ltd, Croydon, CR0 4YY

Pen & Sword Books Ltd incorporates the imprints of
Pen & Sword Aviation, Pen & Sword Maritime,
Pen & Sword Military, Pen & Sword Select, Pen & Sword Military Classics,
Leo Cooper, Wharncliffe Local History

For a complete list of Pen & Sword titles please contact:
PEN & SWORD BOOKS LIMITED
47 Church Street, Barnsley, South Yorkshire, S70 2AS, England.
E-mail: enquiries@pen-and-sword.co.uk
Website: www.pen-and-sword.co.uk

Contents

Acknowledgements

As with previous books, a great big thank you to Anne Coulson for her help in checking the text and to the staff of The Prince Consort's Library and Reading Central Library for their help, kindness and knowledge during the pre-writing stages of this book. While some of the pictures come from books mentioned in the bibliography, many are from my own collection.

Introduction

This book is the second volume in a series that will illustrate life on the Home Front during each year of the war. The many photographs show life through the eyes of those not on the military frontline. The book portrays the life of ordinary citizens and how they experienced the war. Important people appear only as part of the context of everyday life.

This book is not solely about Britain; though the major part of it does record British life I have attempted to show the international commonality of various themes through illustrations from other Allied and enemy countries. Readers may be familiar with some, but most have not been published since the war, and others have never been published.

This a book about the Home Front on an international scale. It is not chronological and, although themed, topics do cross over. Similarly, the difference between being in the forces and being on the Home Front can seem a grey area. It took a long time to train new recruits, and that training was done on the Home Front. In many areas, there were more people in uniform than out of it, a fact that became accepted as part of life.

What was "The Home Front"? There are many interpretations of the phrase: 'the sphere of civilian activity in war'; 'the civilian sector of a nation at war when its armed forces are in combat abroad'; 'the name given to the part of war that was not actively involved in the fighting but which was vital to it'; an 'informal term for the civilian populace of the nation at war as an active support system of their military. Military forces depend on "home front" civilian support services such as factories that build materiel to support the military front'; it 'refers to life in Britain during the war itself'. All of these have elements of truth but none fully describe the range of experiences that shaped the Home Front.

If this book is about life away from the combat zone, then some of what happened on the Home Front cannot be recorded here. For those caught in a Zeppelin raid, the Home Front became a war zone; it was not always 'All quiet on the Home Front' as assumed by the title of one oral history book. In this and the following volumes, I define the Home Front as the totality of the experience of the civilian population in a country affected, directly or indirectly, by the war. As there were considerable numbers of military personnel on the Home Front, interacting with the civilian population, they too are included.

This again needs some examination. The Home Front was not a singular experience. Life in the countryside was different to that in the town or city, the latter being more quickly affected by change. However, life in the Scottish Isles was differed from life in the Kent countryside. Again, life in a coastal town on the east of the country was unlike that on the west. Of course the whole country experienced basic similarities but there were many factors that varied the war's effects. How could a family who lost their only son experience the same war as a neighbour with five serving sons who all returned? What similarities were there between the family of a conscientious objector and one whose father/husband had been killed? Or between an Irish family and a Welsh one?

While there is a common link between all of these examples, what links can be found between Belgian, French, Dutch, German, Japanese or Russian families? All these countries had a Home Front and all were directly affected by the war. There are some obvious differences. Neutral Holland was quickly affected by the war on its borders, and Japan, an isolated Allied Power, fought in the Pacific and escorted convoys, to Europe but was otherwise largely unaffected. Both were unlike the other countries which, despite some differences, were all united by an invasion, long or short, of their Home Fronts.

We can add further layers to the civilian experience of the war through the Home Front. Neutral countries had to defend themselves against possible aggression and were on a war footing which inevitably affected civilian life. They were not at war, so nationals of the warring countries were free to move about as before the war and spying was rife. As safe havens, they became the guardians of hundreds of refugees or prisoners of war. And, as in the warring countries, commodities became short because, once at sea, their ships became targets.

Combatant countries on the continent experienced two types of Home Front, the obvious one being the civilians behind the fighting front. But in an occupied country civilians were behind both sides of the line. All shared the same nationality, but lived on the Home Front, very differently, enduring different constraints.

This book therefore illustrates life on the Home Front for civilians on both sides of the wire.

The Home Fronts in 1915

Very quickly Christmas came - and the war was not over as everyone had hoped. At home and in the front-line it looked to most that it could continue for some time. Well, at least until the 'Big Push' that would end it all. Ironically, both sides felt the same.

In the New Year, the season's mix of gaiety and austerity was quickly replaced with sangfroid, an acceptance that it might not end in 1915. After all Kitchener had told the country it would last at least three years and men were signing up for the duration, regardless of how long that would be. If it didn't end, there was a realisation that life might get harder, and, while there was no shortage of goods yet, some things were more difficult to get hold of than others.

However, the direct impact of the war in Britain was still limited and for most it was a case of 'Business as usual'. This was clearly shown by the large-scale partridge and grouse shoots and the annual Daffodil Show at the Horticultural Hall in Westminster where a new variety was exhibited – the Lord Kitchener. Papers included adverts for the 1915 season at Vichy, France, starting on 1 May. Football matches were well attended as were horse races. This gave rise to one of the most famous posters of the war: a wounded soldier, standing over the bloodied corpse of another soldier, looks into the distance at a crowded race track asking – 'Will they never come?'.

There was no shortage of customers at the Carlton restaurant where it was reported that apart from a few men in khaki and a few limping there was no sign of war. Behind the black-out curtains in Paris it was the same. Until curfew hour, brasseries, theatres, cinemas, night-clubs, concert-halls were busy and the famous Café de Paris was full.

It was the same in Germany where concert-halls, theatres and cinemas were well-attended. In Britain, German music was no longer played, but in Germany, orchestras continued to play French and Italian music and theatres performed Shakespeare. Again, unlike their enemies, the German population had access to British and French newspapers. Naturally *The Times* was the most popular.

In Germany, many sent New Year cards wishing the recipient good luck or expressing the hope for peace and freedom. Both sides felt the same and Reverend Brook-Jackson sent his congregation a hopeful message and something to think about. '1915. We cry you God-speed to the next milestone.

> I sent my soul through the invisible,
> Some letter of that after-life to spell;
> And by and by my soul return'd to me,
> And answer'd "I myself am Heav'n and Hell."
> Remember – God's soldiers wear white uniforms.'

The New Year started with the need for yet more money. On 1 January in Reading there was a collection for POWs. Throughout the year, across the country, there would be many more collections for a multitude of different organisations. In Britain and France, 'flag days' became the norm for collecting money, while in Germany collection boxes were more common. In 1915 collections occurred after a press announcement. By the end of the war, there was a strict rota with hard-and-fast rules, otherwise no collection was permitted.

The biggest single issue that Britain faced during the year was recruitment. Unlike France and Germany, where men expected to be called-up, until the end of the year, enlistment in Britain remained voluntary. While manpower was becoming short on the Home Front it was even more so in France where universal conscription drew every fit man aged between eighteen and forty-seven into the armed forces. By mid-1915, 5,444,000 French men had been drafted.

After the initial rush the number of volunteers fell even though the government constantly asked for more men and the local papers published small ads to encourage enlistment. Many methods were used to try and encourage men to volunteer. Recruiting rallies were held, volunteers marched through towns and cities to encourage others, concerts were held - and white feathers were handed out. Shame was a powerful weapon in the arsenal of the recruiter. Even the King became involved when he sent out a message published in papers nationwide. He addressed it 'To My People' and wrote: 'At this grave moment in the struggle between my people and a highly organised enemy who has transgressed the Laws of Nations and changed the ordinance that binds civilized Europe together, I appeal to you…I ask you, men of all classes, to come forward voluntarily and take your share in the fight…' George R.I.

In areas where there were insufficient men for local units, adverts were placed in neighbouring areas to poach men. A typical example were the "Oxford Shiners", a Royal Garrison Artillery unit. Based in Oxford, they tried to take recruits from Caversham, a northern suburb of Reading which until 1911 had been part of Oxfordshire.

Women were used as another way of getting men to enlist. Many were happy to hand out white feathers to those they felt should be in khaki. The Reading Citizens' Recruiting Committee published the following in order to encourage women as recruiters: 'Don't fail to urge eligible men of military age, especially single men, to enlist at once; Don't hesitate to send the names and addresses of those who should join to the Recruiting Officer…Your letter will be treated confidentially. Don't put obstacles in the way of those who are anxious to enlist.' Later the discussion would revolve around compulsion or a continuation of the volunteer system. By December there would be no option. The only question was whether to volunteer before compulsion or just wait and see if you would be conscripted.

Prosperity caused by the war also helped to keep men out of the forces. An increase in employment meant that unemployment was very low. The demand for labour, caused by increased production and many men enlisting, pushed both wages and prices up. Strikes and disputes fell. Britain was in a boom situation, where it was estimated each man at the front needed three civilian workers to equip and maintain him.

Increased armament production was hampered by the labour shortage, a shortage caused by skilled men enlisting and by the numbers employed in apparently less essential work. As a result, orders for ships could not be fulfilled and armaments companies had to employ women. The problem was compounded by many being unwilling to move to where the work was. The new coalition government would solve these problems as a matter of urgency with production changes during the year affecting the level of efficiency in British factories.

During the shell scandal, British firms had been producing about 700 a day compared to 250,000 in Germany and nearly as many in France. As a result of the powers under the Munitions Act, Lloyd George replaced 'the wasteful inefficiencies and the old piecemeal industrial methods that largely depended on private initiative' with 'a system of national direction and compulsion.' With these changes 'the nation's plants, factories and civilian work-force' would be 'marshalled and co-ordinated into a gigantic arsenal for the paramount task of producing the guns and shells sufficient to meet the voracious and ever-growing demands of the battlefronts.'

In France, which had lost 6% of her territory, 14% of her industrial work-force, 12% of her soil and 21% of her manufacturing labour, these grave losses imposed severe industrial and labour problems. There, unlike Britain, they were quickly addressed and by July 1915 75% of pre-war establishments were back at work. Extra workers had been found by the temporary release of soldiers, utilising the unemployed, refugees and foreign and colonial workers, while intensifying night and extra shifts. 'Women were employed everywhere and disabled soldiers were trained in war work.' Even this was not enough, and 300,000 skilled workers were released from the forces for the arms factories and coal mines, a number eventually increased to 500,000.

Taking a leaf from the French, 40,000 skilled workers were recalled from the colours; but this was not a complete solution. To overcome the shortage, the government had to secure special agreement with unions to allow the dilution of skilled labour with semi-and un-skilled workers. In order to make these changes work, defaulting workers were tried by Munition Courts for offences such as leaving employment, lateness and striking. Remarkably, these radical readjustments did not cause widespread problems. There were only 674 trade disputes in the year, the fewest since 1910.

These changes were accompanied by a change in people's attitude, particularly to manpower. Workers were called on to make greater efforts and, in speeches, sermons and press articles, the public were urged to reduce manpower needs. Economy in food and dress was instilled. As a result, shop hours were reduced, people carried their own purchases, luxury spending fell and some stores closed branches. People travelled less and fewer cars were bought – although papers continued to advertise them. Even the very well-off fell in line, and, where possible, managed, to some extent, to do without their chauffeurs, gardeners and gamekeepers. But this did not solve the manpower needs of the army.

It was the same in France with munitions output taking priority. Wages rose and some families brought home weekly wages in a day. New factories were created and older ones switched to war work. One issue that did arise was caused by the use of temporarily-released soldiers. They received little more than starvation pay for their work, while released ex-soldiers and civilians earned high rates: in one factory, temporary workers, quartered in barracks, receiving no family allowance because they were not at the front, received ¼ franc a day, while in a nearby factory, demobilised troops, living at home, received fifteen francs for the same work. So difficult were the working conditions, just as in British factories, that some men asked to be sent back to the front.

As in Britain, war industries boomed while less essential industries declined, creating shortages, often for simple essentials like matches. Although wine was a staple of the French diet, production fell because of the lack of skilled employees. However, unlike Britain, France had access to a large external labour market. Paris, in particular, saw a vast influx of mostly middle-aged men from Belgium, Italy and Spain - so many that the pre-war population almost doubled. On the outskirts, new hutments steadily grew into small townships.

As men disappeared from the job market, women rallied in ever-increasing numbers to take their place. 'Besides taking on a host of civilian jobs normally done by men, they were to be absorbed in their thousands into Lloyd George's war factories.' Their chance came in March 'when the Board of Trade issued an appeal to all women willing to take "paid employment of any kind" in trade, commerce or agriculture to enter their names on a Register of Women for War Service at any employment exchange.' Each woman employed would naturally release a man for the front.

The response was phenomenal. 124,000 enrolled and many quickly took the place of men in government offices censoring, working in the census department, War Office and Post Office. 'Hundreds took jobs in the clothing, tailoring and leather trades, as gardeners and agricultural hands, laboratory assistants…tram and bus conductors, bank clerks, ticket-collectors on the tubes and railways, plumbers' assistants, milk and newspaper deliverers, gas-meter readers.' Very soon there were few occupations they had not made inroads into. Women were determined to contribute and, in pouring rain in mid-July, paraded through London on the 'Women's right to serve' march, carrying placards that clearly showed their aim: 'We demand the right to serve.'

Initially those women employed in munition factories came from other industries, but the demand for munitions meant employing thousands who had never worked in a factory. Those employed included many 'ladies' with time to spare and many who were in domestic service - as many as 400,000 throughout the war.

Naturally the employment of women was not welcomed by everyone. There was opposition from Trade Unionists because they felt it would affect men's wages. Some believed that some jobs could not be done by women, 'the weaker sex', and, even with a chronic shortage of labourers many farmers were loath to employ them. The other side of the coin was that employers saw them as cheap labour. Even in government munitions factories, they generally earned less even when doing the same job as men.

Working conditions were often primitive, even in the new government factories. Many lacked basic facilities and by the end of the year it was noted that the health of women workers was being affected and that normal family life was impossible for many: with mother and older children away making munitions, the young, left at home, were neglected. In France, while children were wearing themselves out in the fields because of the lack of labour, in some factories efforts were made to help mothers by providing crèches, nursing rooms and nurseries.

For all the problems, women now had greater freedom than ever before. Shedding old inhibitions, women used language that would have shocked their mothers, took to smoking and drinking in public houses and using cosmetics. Clothing styles changed as well, with long dresses and camisoles being replaced by short skirts and brassieres, soon to be followed by trousers.

Greater freedom and increased wages were blamed for increased sexual laxity and for the rise in drunkenness. While the former raised concerns about large numbers of 'war babies', as a result of one-night stands, the later was seen by the government as more dangerous than the Germans. When week-end indulgence led to absenteeism on Monday and a one-day Bank Holiday turned into a week, the government acted. The King signed the pledge as an example and the government established a Central Control Board to regulate drink in military and munition-making areas. Opening hours were reduced, treating became an offence, beer strength was reduced, many public house licences were not renewed, the purchase of spirits was forbidden apart from very carefully controlled times on Monday to Friday, and duties were increased. To further reduce consumption and intoxication, wounded soldiers could not be served alcohol and women were no longer able to purchase any alcoholic drink that was to be consumed on the premises before mid-day.

These measures did reduce drink-related offences but the local papers continued to report cases of drunkenness in both sexes. Typical court appearances included intoxication while holding on to a lamp post or iron railings, abusing the Police Constable who found them in the small hours unable to move, or simply just walking up and down the main street while drunk.

Sexual laxity was easy to explain. 'Life was less than cheap; it was thrown away. The religious teaching that the body was the temple of the Holy Ghost could mean little or nothing to those who saw it mutilated and destroyed in millions by Christian nations engaged in war. All moral standards were held for a short moment and irretrievably lost. Little wonder that the old ideals of chastity and self-control in sex were, for many, also lost.' There was also a feeling of this might be the last chance: with young men alive today and dead tomorrow, and young women reading casualty lists, many felt that, if they 'did not seize the experience at once, they knew that for many of them it would elude them for ever.' And, of course, there were few chaperones available to prevent it.

By the end of the year, drinking facilities had been severely reduced and curtailed. This control had a positive effect on the population. Not only did the number of convictions for drunkenness fall, but the lack of supply meant that many had money in their pockets at the end of the week. This resulted in the purchase of better and healthier foods in many working-class households.

Moral laxity and drink problems were also noted in France, especially in Paris, where every woman was described as living a fast life and people believed that all females wanted a man about the-house. At the same time, an outbreak of syphilis was reported. To reduce drink-related problems, absinthe was banned, hours of opening fixed, soldiers prohibited from buying wine and spirits except at certain times and women forbidden to do so. Women and youths under eighteen could only be served with the weakest alcoholic drink.

It was the same in Germany. Munich was said to be full of fashionable prostitutes - cocottes, the largest hotel in the city had a special tea-room exclusively for officers and cocottes and 'dances *sans voiles* were all the vogue.' The behaviour of many officers' wives was classed as being 'truly scandalous'.

Many in this country saw the National Registration Act in July as a further whittling away of British freedoms. Under this Act everyone between the ages of fifteen and sixty-five had to carry a registration card that provided basic personal details. Failure to register could be punished by a £20 fine and three months' hard labour.

The next step in removing British freedoms was to be conscription. Fortunately, popular feeling was that it was necessary to secure victory. However, the government tried a final method to gain men on a voluntary basis. In October, Lord Derby, Under-Secretary for War was appointed Director of Recruitment. The first task was to canvass the nation's manpower. Using the National Register, every man between eighteen and forty-one was asked to attest and enlist when called for. Men would be split into two groups, single and married, and then further sub-divided according to age. The call-up would start with younger single men, leaving the married men until all single men had been enlisted. Some workers were exempt – the starred occupations: some branches of agriculture, coal miners, the Merchant Navy, munitions, public utilities and railwaymen. When registration closed in December, the result was a failure – out of two million single men, only 343,000 had attested.

Compulsion was now seen as necessary but as it came closer opposition became more vocal: pacifists, anti-conscription groups and conscientious objectors spoke out against it. With popular pro-war sentiment running high, they received little sympathy for their views and any peace meeting run by them was held to be the work of German agents. However, unless they broke the law, they were safe to hold their views until the introduction of conscription and the sitting of the tribunals that would decide whether a man would be enlisted, deferred, or granted exemption because of their trade or belief.

In Germany, the autocratic government was organising the civilian population more rigorously and efficiently than either Britain or France. Neither of these countries was yet on a full war footing, but by the spring of 1915 Germany was, thanks to Walter Rathenau. When founding the War Raw Materials Department in August 1914, he compiled an inventory of the nation's resources. He then created War Industries Companies which commandeered materials and made sure they got to the intended producer. By spring, when it was all handed over to the government, he was able to report 'that the blockade had been defeated and that a scarcity of essential materials no longer threatened the fate of the war.' Germany war-production was in top gear and seemed capable of matching her enemy's.

For both sides there was one common issue – food. It, for most, brought the reality of the war directly into the home, clearly shown by the panic buying only months previously, before government maximum prices stopped the rush.

Britain was in a better position with regard to food and was able to abandon price-fixing and let the markets deal with themselves. However, the German submarine blockade that started in February would ultimately have tremendous repercussions on food availability, making the free market untenable. But rationing as in Germany was a long way in the future.

There were no actual food restrictions in Britain but this was not the case in France or Germany. The French restrictions were more symbolic: the banning of the French roll in Paris. Meanwhile Germany was already producing 'War Bread', flour adulterated with rye and potato flour, even though the harvest had been above average. In November 1914, the hours for baking and selling bread were regulated and in Berlin 'bread constables' were appointed to protect bakers in case of riots. However, there was a silver lining for the German population. A shortage of fodder resulted in orders to slaughter large numbers of cattle and pigs, releasing large quantities of meat and sausages onto the market.

The only shortages so far in France were flour, because of the army's needs, and sugar because the harvest had been below average. Although prices had risen and there was some risk of shortages caused by U-boats, in general there was little difference between the food available in 1915 and that before the war.

In January Germany introduced bread rationing, with each citizen being issued with a bread card that provided a daily allowance of 225 grams 'with modifications according to age, sex, type of work and so on.' The card had to be presented to the baker and when eating bread in a restaurant. Although the mass slaughter provided large quantities of meat, this situation did not last long and soon there were shortages. As a result, meat, along with potatoes, became carefully controlled. There was little fresh meat and prices rose.

With 20% of food coming from abroad, and much labour in the armed forces, the population were simply told to eat less. The message was spread by meetings, exhibitions, slogans posted on walls, and by clergy and schoolmasters. There was also a drive to reduce food waste with special pails to collect it for feeding animals. Steeply rising prices were controlled by government-set maximum prices.

To control grain supplies, the Imperial Grain Office was formed. As other food became scarce, more Imperial Offices were set up to regulate each food. Soon fats, fruit, meat, potatoes, sugar, spirits and vegetables were regulated. Despite this control, prices continued to rise. In May prices were reported to be 65% above those of July 1914. To help the population, large cities set up People's Kitchens and workers' canteens, an idea that would be adopted by Britain in due course but not for some considerable time. Cultivating any spare ground was another way in which output could be increased, again an idea that Britain developed later in the war.

Although there were butter riots and a shortage of milk in the autumn, and everyone blamed someone else for any shortage, the truth was that Germany was not short of food. Shortages could be made good by buying American exports to neutral governments so the British blockade initially made little impression on food supplies.

Britain and France had no form of rationing; they had free markets to respond to needs. While Britain held four months' food reserves at the beginning of the year, this did not prevent steep price rises. Costs were so high that Labour MPs in a Parliamentary debate in February claimed that many labourers were only getting one good meal a week. Although the government was aware of the price increases, government inaction was justified on rather strange grounds: the 'rises were no worse than the ones brought by the aftermath of the Franco-Prussian war of 1870.'

'By July average prices had increased by 34% compared with August 1914. Meat cost 40% more, fish 60%, bread nearly 40%, flour 45%. Sugar, which had risen by 68%, was taken under government control.' As a result more vegetables and salads were eaten.

Average rises masked the cost to the working classes who usually purchased the cheaper cuts. 'Neck of mutton had previously cost between 2½d to 3d a pound but by 1915 the lowest grade of this cut – scrag of mutton – was fetching from 4½d to 6d a pound while brisket had risen from around 5d a pound to 9d.' Fish had become so scarce that the Archbishop of Westminster allowed parishioners to eat flesh on Fridays instead.

This was closely paralleled in France where due to the loss of the sugar beet factories in the north, the price of sugar rose sharply. However, unlike Britain, there was no government control. Prices increased, particularly in Paris, where the average increase was estimated at 300%.

Industry needed coal, as did households. In France and Germany the call-up reduced the number of miners. The French had a second problem: its coalfields were in the north and many had been lost in the German advance. British coalfields were also affected because of the large numbers that joined up, estimated to be around 14% by the start of the year. Each country also had transportation problems because of the need to move military equipment. As a result, like food, coal prices went up. By February best Derbyshire coal had risen 20%, resulting in the British government taking steps to curb profits and limit price rises.

The real shortage in Germany was of raw materials, particularly copper. While Britain and France could purchase these overseas, the British blockade effectively cut Germany off from such supplies. With demand high, householders sold spare copper goods for melting down for munitions use. Even copper roofs disappeared.

The war quickly changed the face of French and British politics. In May, following the shell scandal, Asquith announced the formation of a coalition government and the creation of a Ministry of Munitions. A veteran Socialist, Aristide Briand, replaced Viviani in October, instilling fresh encouragement into the French people with a coalition government. In Germany, after backing the war effort as long as it was defensive, the Socialists, who now realised they had been duped, opposed further war credits. In June and July they went as far as to declare that the masses wanted peace. Although the largest party, 'their protests amounted to little' as did also the power of the Reichstag. Real power in Germany lay with the Emperor and Supreme War Lord, and his Imperial Chancellor and appointed Secretaries of State, none of whom were in the Reichstag.

At the same time as the Socialists were voicing opposition to the war, there was a demonstration by about 500 women outside the Reichstag, railing against the failure of the German Ambassador in Rome to keep Italy out of the war. They also grumbled about high prices, called for the return of their men - and complained that the whipped cream was not as good as before the war. No mention of the assembly appeared in the papers nor of one in November when a group of a few hundred women marched down the Unter den Linden chanting 'Peace, Peace'. This march was broken up by police armed with swords. They arrested the ringleaders who received short terms of imprisonment. There was a further peace demonstration in December. Again no mention was made in the press.

Demonstrations were by no means unique to Germany. In Glasgow, 15,000 protested against a 20% increase in rents. As a result the government passed legislation that fixed rents at pre-war levels.

Both France and Germany were quick to show off the spoils of war with displays in Paris and triumphal marches and displays in Germany. Towns across Germany displayed the weapons their men had captured. In Leipzig, the British field guns on display had been captured by Saxon troops. In France the emphasis was more on the quantity, with much material being shown in the war museum in Les Invalides. Many museums re-opened and held war-themed displays ranging from tapestries from Rheims to objets d'art from Belgium. Britain did not start to show captured equipment until newspapers started publishing letters complaining about this.

On 21 December 1914, German aircraft had bombed Dover. This was the first air-raid on British territory and would be followed by many more in 1915. Although Zeppelin raids were often inaccurate and haphazard in their results, they did cause considerable inconvenience for many cities. Moon timetables were published that showed the most likely days for an attack. On possible attack nights, many householders left their homes and decamped to safer towns, or spent the night in a park or in the countryside.

The first successful raid on Britain took place on the night of 19–20 January 1915 when two Zeppelins targeted Humberside. Strong winds took them off course and they dropped their bombs on Great Yarmouth, Sheringham, King's Lynn and the surrounding villages. Four people were killed and 16 injured. The raid tied in with people's fears of spies, nine of whom would shot during the year: alarmist stories appeared about car headlights being used to guide Zeppelins to their targets, and a rumour spread that a Zeppelin was operating from a concealed base in the Lake District. It also linked with propaganda stories about how barbaric the Germans were with their scant regard for civilian life.

Naturally the raid caused considerable concern across the country. The *Daily Mail* editorial probably expressed the views of many. 'They have been slain for no military purpose. Yarmouth is not a fortified town…the Germans have acted at Yarmouth as they acted at Hartlepool and Scarborough and as their troops have acted in countless places in Belgium and France.' The important point in the editorial was that 'it grows clearer with each month of the war that the immunity which non-combatants away from the actual scene of the fighting formerly enjoyed has passed away.'

Over the year there were a further nineteen raids resulting in 455 people injured and 177 dying. Although there had been German raids against coastal targets before the raids, it was the Zeppelin that brought the front-line to the Home Front. One incident emphasised this clearly.

During an air raid on Southend and district on 10 May, the Germans dropped a postcard. It was a prophecy: 'You English. We have come, and we will come again soon. Kill or cure. German.' By the end of the year, the death toll from air raids amounted to 209, small change compared to the 2,371 lives that had been lost from the sinking of British merchant vessels and minute compared to the losses at the front. Small but disturbing. 'As a young officer, home on leave was heard to say, during a raid on London's theatre area, "it's no business to happen here".'

Paris was the target for the first Zeppelin raid against France. In March a single airship attempted to bomb the city; many slept through the raid, others thought it was a fire. Caught in the searchlights from the Arc de Triomphe and the Eiffel Towe, it turned north and disappeared. There were no reported casualties. Other French cities were less lucky. Nancy, close to the front, had frequent air raids.

Raids such as these and the sinking of the Lusitania had a dramatic effect on many. While there had been some anti-German feeling since the start of the war and outbursts against some citizens of German origin, the bombing and sinking of the Lusitania brought it to a head. As a result, in many affected areas there were riots, looting and damage to property thought to be German, even if the owners were naturalised or second-generation. Hull and Liverpool were two cities in which feelings ran high, the former after the bombing, the latter as a result of many of the crew of the Lusitania coming from Liverpool.

In Hull many of the shops attacked belonged to German pork butchers. Some of these had lived in the city for many years and were part of the community. This did not stop the attacks, and neither did the crowds differentiate between those who were naturalised and those who were second-or third-generation British citizens who just happened to have German names. One such family were the Hohenreins: one son was in the British Army, another was interned in Germany as a British citizen and the father had been born in Britain. All this was irrelevant to rioters.

After the sinking, the King showed his feelings by striking the names of the German Emperor, the Emperor of Austria-Hungary, and many other German royals, including his cousin the Duke of Cumberland, from the Roll of the Knights of the Garter.

Naturally, with a greater foreign population, the worst excesses were in London. Fanned by the press, especially by Horatio Bottomley, there was outrage that thousands of German aliens were still at large and stockbrokers marched to the Houses of Parliament to protest about them. At the Stock Exchange and Baltic Exchange, German merchants and brokers were expelled and in Smithfield Market German butchers were turned out by their colleagues. As in Hull and Liverpool, crowds attacked and looted German shops in the East End with German pianos being thrown into the street and used to accompany the singing of patriotic songs. Within a week of the sinking and riots, the government acted. All enemy aliens still free would be interned, with some exceptions, or, if over military age be repatriated. This would also apply to women and children. Naturalised citizens would remain free.

Public opinion was hardening and becoming more belligerent to the enemy. The execution of Edith Cavell was a further propaganda victory for Britain. It further stoked civilian anger and stirred Home Front workers to work even harder. To many it was further proof of the depravity of the German people. It was now their war but they were going to let it interfere as little as possible with their lives. It was 'Business as usual'.

Then once again it was Christmas, the second of the war, a Christmas many thought they would never see. Instead of victory, each country could see another year of struggle ahead. In Britain, war or no war, it would be business as usual in the stores. While it would be a quieter festive season than usual, the bottom line was still money. In most towns and cities trade 'far exceeded expectations', town centres were as busy as before the war and many seemed to have forgotten that there was a war.

Eager to join in the rush, Hill's Rubber Co. advertised its wares in a suitable vein. 'This is a utilitarian age, and especially at the present time it is necessary that money should be wisely spent and not frittered away.' Making the sales really topical, they were 'selling goods suitable for wounded soldiers, hot water bottles, air pillows and cushions for relief, rubber pads for sticks and crutches. Rubber overshoes and boots for nurses who go out in all weathers. For the little ones, unbreakable dolls and animals and rubber funniosities (sic) such as "dying Kaisers", pigs, monkeys, flying sausages, glum faces, balloons and plate-lifters.'

To aid husbands with their Christmas shopping, a large department store had some useful suggestions. 'Furs are always acceptable. We cannot all give diamonds for Christmas gifts, but a set of really nice furs is within reach of the most modest purse – at least, it is at Hedgecocks. The furs that are now in fashion are not expensive when you consider that fashionable sets are priced from 21s and upwards to, say, £8.8.0d, it is evident that a gift of furs will fit with whatever you wish to spend. Squirrel, Red and Black Fox, handsome black wolf, Coney and Musquash furs are all well represented at Hedgecocks.' For those on a lower budget, there was a great range of imitation sets from 4s 11d to 19s 11d the set, and of course the Christmas staples of gloves, scarves and handkerchiefs.

Colebrook & Co., butchers, were pleased to let their customers know they had secured supplies for the Christmas trade, equal in quality to former years. While proud to record that over 100 of their employees were serving and that many more had attested, it had not been possible to replace them. With a greatly reduced staff they earnestly requested the placing of orders for Christmas fare as early as possible so they could 'give all possible attention to their valued orders.'

In Britain, Christmas was quieter but there had still been a festive mood. The situation was different in Germany. Few were in a celebratory mood. Everywhere were the sad reminders of loss, with many women wearing black. 'Devout Roman Catholics sought consolation at Midnight Mass. A typical chapel was filled with wounded soldiers, nurses, nuns and pale, sorrowing women, praying for the dying and dead, and for themselves that they might never again "spend such a Christmas of anguish and suspense".' While British shops had been filled with goods and promised the usual annual sales in the New Year, such sales were forbidden in Germany. Similarly, British butchers were able to fulfil their customers' orders, as long as they came in early enough, while there were shortages of much traditional Christmas fare in German towns and cities.

A more subdued Christmas quickly ran into the New Year. An English newspaper's editorial about the year could easily have been written by either side. 'The war has cast its shadow over all public and private activities during the year, affecting in innumerable ways our corporate and individual life. Few indeed are the families that have not one or more members in the Army or Navy, many of whom, alas! have laid down their lives for their country.' People on the Home Front wanted it to end but many knew that it would not do so in 1916.

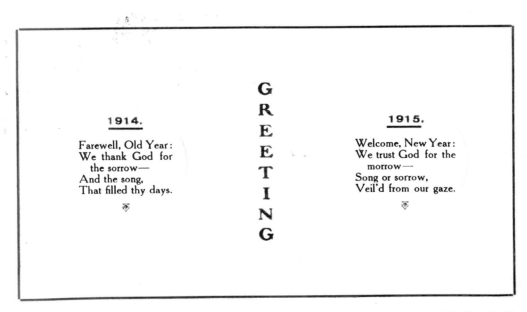

<table>
<tr><td>

1914.

Farewell, Old Year:
We thank God for
the sorrow—
And the song,
That filled thy days.

</td><td>

**G
R
E
E
T
I
N
G**

</td><td>

1915.

Welcome, New Year:
We trust God for the
morrow—
Song or sorrow,
Veil'd from our gaze.

</td></tr>
</table>

GWHF15_001. New Year cards were not common in Britain. This is a rather uninspiring example to start the New Year, thanking God for the pain and the pleasure of what may come in 1915.

Motto for 1915

Fight the Good Fight.

GWHF15_002. A more uplifting home-made card for the coming year.

GWHF15_003. The New Year card was more common in Germany. This example proffers what all on both sides were wishing for: Peace and prosperity in the New Year.

GWHF15_004. Soldiers of a Service Battalion of the Berkshire Regiment celebrating the New Year courtesy of the inhabitants of Reading.

Section 1
Recruiting and departure

GWHF15_006. To show their patriotism many households placed cards in the front window to show how many of the household were serving in the forces. This household, somewhere in southern England has six serving.

GWHF15_007. Any method was used to try and get men to enlist. This march was aimed at shaming other children into coercing their male relatives to join the fathers of the march.

GWHF15_011. Many recruitment rallies took place in Trafalgar Square, usually before large crowds. This is Captain William Short, the King's trumpeter, sounding "Fall In" during a recruitment drive.

GWHF15_010. There were regular recruitment drives in Australia. This crowd are gathered around the entrance to the recruiting office in Melbourne Town Hall.

FOR GOD, KING and COUNTRY.
BERMONDSEY'S OWN BATTALION.
3rd 22nd-QUEEN'S.

2. JAMAICA RD.

TO-DAY,
Bermondsey's Own
a LONDON REGIMENT THE QUEEN'S
RECRUITS URGENTLY NEEDED

WHY DELAY!

Der kleinste u. größte
Kriegsfreiwilliger
1. Rekr. De
1. Ers. Ba
7. Inf. Re
=1915
Bayreuth

GWHF15_015. The sinking of the Lusitania was a boon for recruiting sergeants who offered potential revenge for the murder of the innocents on board. These three are potential recruits for the 22nd London Regiment.

GWHF15_009. Although Germany had conscription, not all men had previously served before the war. For many reasons, not just health, only a certain percentage were taken for the draft. At the outbreak of the war many of them volunteered, like Kitchener's men, and joined Recruit Depots as War Volunteers. This shows the biggest and smallest volunteers for the 1st Replacement Battalion of 7 Infantry Regiment, then in training at Bayreuth. It is unlikely that the smaller of the two would have joined the British Army, even as a Bantam.

GWHF15_012. A common method of, hopefully, instilling martial spirit into the men in the crowd was a route march through busy town and city centres. This is a battalion of the Berkshire Regiment marching through Reading.

GWHF15_020. Meetings were
wherever there was space for a [
An Indian officer is seen here
addressing a meeting in the Str[
How effective he would have be[
such a class-based society can o[
surmised.

GWHF15_017. Lord Kitchener personally addressed meetings in
order to boost recruitment. Here he is talking to a crowd outside the
London Guildhall.

GWHF15_019. The execution of Edith Cavell aided recruiting
as did the sinking of the Lusitania. Here a recruiting officer is
appealing to the crowd for avengers to come forward.

GWHF15_018. A photograph from a German magazine published in 1915 captioned
'Miss Lorriane, a well-known English actress, is in London for the recruiting drive.'

GWHF15_021. A rally outside the Town Hall at Johannesburg on 23 November drew a crowd of over eleven thousand. After a stirring address, hundreds signed on for service in German East Africa.

GWHF15_023. Everyone loves a military band concert. In front of an enormous military poster in Aldwych, a recruiting band is playing a selection of patriotic tunes to passers-by.

GWHF15_022. There was no explanation for the rush to enlist given in the original caption. This is a scene outside a recruiting office in Ottawa.

GWHF15_025. While the patriotic spirit was in their blood, there were recruiting officers ready to swear men in to the army before their ardour waned. A new recruit being sworn in in Trafalgar Square, during a rally, in front of the crowd, in the hope of encouraging others to join him.

GWHF15_024. Two youthful men proudly show off their newly acquired Derby armbands that show they are prepared to join the army when it needs them, but not before then.

GWHF15_027. The direct approach to join a specific battalion shown here by the 24th Middlesex. Recruiting outside St. Paul's, they were appealing for 500 new recruits.

GWHF15_028. Even the Lord Mayor's parade in November was turned into a recruiting campaign. This is a Royal Navy mounted light anti-aircraft gun.

GWHF15_026. 'Among the many ingenious devices resorted to to convince the hesitant eligible of his country's needs was the one illustrated…The blackboard was placed outside the Royal Naval Division office in the Strand. A curious and likely recruit, reading the notice, would see himself reflected in the mirror, whereupon the business-like looking handyman would help him to make up his mind.'

GWHF15_029. As the December cut-off point for voluntary enlistment into the Derby Scheme approached, there were queues at recruiting offices reminiscent of the early months of the war.

GWHF15_030. Mass enlistment during the final days or hours of the Derby scheme.

GWHF15_032. Very soon after the scheme closed some of the early groups, the unmarried younger men, were called up. When they received their papers they went to a depot where they handed in their armbands, joined the army and received their uniform.

GWHF15_034. Derby men inspecting the newly posted proclamation outside Mansion House calling up the first four Derby groups to the colours.

GWHF15_035. When they reported, because they were volunteers, they were allowed to choose their regiment, with of course help from sergeants keen to get the best for their regiment.

GWHF15_036. Derby men, newly enlisted at the recruiting office in Jamaica Road, Bermondsey, marching off to their training camp.

GWHF15_038. In November, Winston Churchill, having left office, set off to join his regiment at the front.

GWHF15_039. A newly-trained replacement battalion sets off for the front while a few well-wishers give them a send-off.

GWHF15_042. Men of a Royal Berkshire Regiment Service Battalion waving farewell as they leave for further training on Salisbury Plain.

GWHF15_043. An Australian hospital ship leaving Sydney for overseas service carrying the 3rd Australian General Hospital. The streamers were fixed at both ends so that when the boat left the well-wishers and men aboard could keep a part of the streamer as a souvenir.

GWHF15_044. When a division was ready to leave for the front they were inspected, whenever possible by the King. He sits, facing the marching troops.

His Majesty the King inspects troops on Salisbury Plain.

Section 2
Getting ready for war and Home Defence

GWHF15_049. Ununiformed men digging trenches somewhere in London. These were part of the Great War version of Dad's Army, the National Guard. At first unofficially used by the army for guarding bridges and providing general manpower, they eventually became part of the official military establishment.

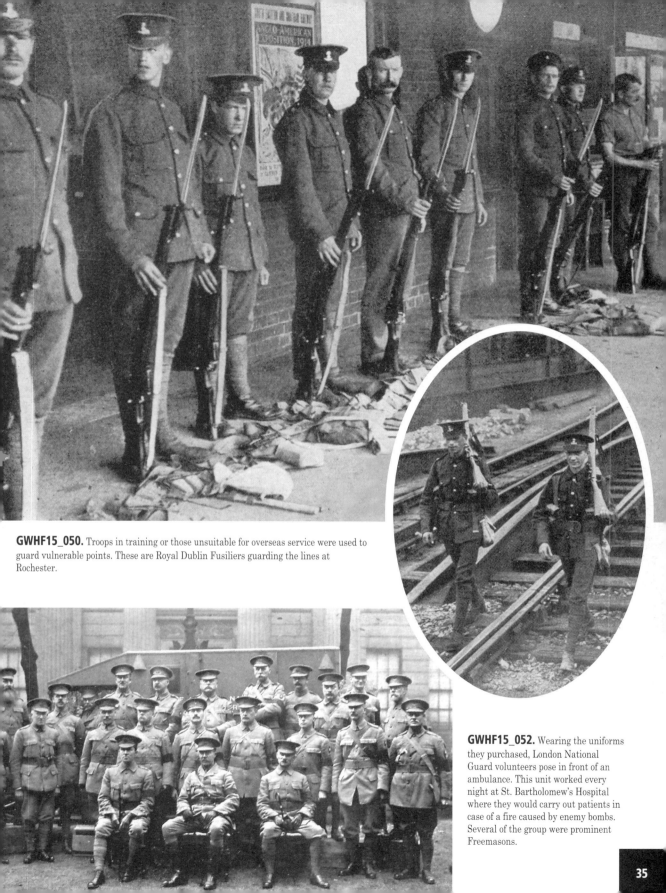

GWHF15_050. Troops in training or those unsuitable for overseas service were used to guard vulnerable points. These are Royal Dublin Fusiliers guarding the lines at Rochester.

GWHF15_052. Wearing the uniforms they purchased, London National Guard volunteers pose in front of an ambulance. This unit worked every night at St. Bartholomew's Hospital where they would carry out patients in case of a fire caused by enemy bombs. Several of the group were prominent Freemasons.

GWHF15_053. With new huts being rapidly built across Salisbury Plain, many units, like the Royal Berks who had been quartered in Reading, were able to move and finish their training.

GWHF15_054. Both sides use any method they could invent to get money from the public either to support the war effort or for charities. These model trenches a Berlin Park could only be entered if the visitor had paid an entrance fee which was given to the Red Cross.

GWHF15_055. In Germany, youths coming up to military service age joined organisations that taught them skills that would be handy when they joined the military. These youths are at a naval training school.

GWHF15_058. A group of older men, probably ones who had not done their initial conscript service, pose prior to leaving for the front where they would replace losses in Infantry Regiment 162.

GWHF15_066. Two common sights around Britain in 1915 were soldiers, now in full uniform, and adverts for men to join a specific unit like the one here wanting men for a Bantam Battalion, a Field Artillery Regiment and the 34th Divisional Ammunition Column.

GWHF15_070. In parallel with the free refreshment stall for military personnel was the free overnight accommodation provided in many towns and cities. This hut was built quickly in Euston Square to accommodate twenty-three soldiers for the night. It was not designed for soldiers to stay in, just a night's sleep as they went on or returned from leave.

GWHF15_075. Smaller towns often provided recreation rooms for the soldiers stationed in the area. Often they were in buildings of a religious nature such as church halls or non-conformist churches. This is in the Friends' Meeting House in Saffron Walden.

GWHF15_074. The inside of the Euston Square hut.

GWHF15_071. Lloyd George and his wife opening a new refreshment stall for men in the forces.

Section 3
Raids and U-boats

GWHF15_076. There was a reward of £500 for the first merchantman to sink a submarine. This is Captain William Bell of the collier *Thordis* which rammed a U-boat on 28 February. The collision left a large hole in the ship which had to put into Weymouth. He was awarded the DSC for the sinking and given a commission in the Royal Naval Reserve as a Lieutenant. He and his crew shared a prize of over £600 for the sinking, although German sources stated that the damage was inconsiderable and the submarine had reached port safely.

GWHF15_077. Within a short distance of Folkestone harbour, the hospital ship *Anglia*, returning from France with wounded on board, struck a mine on 17 November. In total 129 soldiers and crew were lost. The boat going to her rescue, the collier *Lusitania*, also struck a mine and sank.

GWHF15_081. A torpedoed cargo steamer in dry-dock for repairs.

GWHF15_078. Seven of the survivors from the sinking of the *Anglia* outside the County of London War Hospital.

GWHF15_087. Some of the coffins being taken to the temporary mortuary for the recovered bodies from the *Lusitania*.

GWHF15_088. Carrying a recovered American body to the mortuary in Queenstown.

GWHF15_082. The steam ships *Indian City* and *Headlands* were torpedoed just a few miles from the Isles of Scilly by Captain Weddigen's U-boat. There were no casualties and the crews made their way to St. Mary's with the help of a local ship.

GWHF15_093. A *Lusitania* survivor still wearing his life vest.

GWHF15_094. Captain Turner, master of the *Lusitania*, survived after he was swept from the bridge by holding on to a chair for three hours.

GWHF15_097. Liverpool men avenged the Liverpudlians lost on the *Lusitania* by wrecking Ge[rman] shops in the town.

GWHF15_095. Two younger survivors of the sinking.

GWHF15_099. Rioting crowds in the East End of London ransacking a German-owned shop.

GWHF15_100. The sinking of the *Lusitania* had effects beyond Britain. This is a German shop in South Africa.

GWHF15_102. Air raids were also a threat to the Home Front. This is Campanile di San Marco in Venice, sandbagged against bomb damage.

GWHF15_103. Paris was protected by anti-aircraft guns and searchligh

GWHF15_107. The remains of the ceiling of the
Church of Santa Maria Dei Scalzi in Venice after an
Austrian air-raid.

GWHF15_106. Part of a Parisian anti-aircraft battery with observer
and range finder in the background.

GWHF15_108. 'A just reprisal as well as an attack of military value' read the original caption. 'On June 15th, twenty-three French aviators flew over Karlsrühe and dropped some hundred and thirty bombs on the city, thereby carrying out a just reprisal for Zeppelin raids on Paris. This photograph shows a street of houses near the barracks, which were set alight by the bomb explosions.'

GWHF15_109. 'Death and destruction by bomb in the Piazza delle Erbe' in Verona. The attack was made on Sunday morning after mass when the piazza was a favourite gathering place for friends. The casualties were light considering the number of people present.

GWHF15_110. Closer to home, this shows the effect [of a] bomb on a house in South Street, Southend, in May. Over 100 bombs were dropped on the town and one person killed.

Presented by
"The Kaiser"
Sept. 12th 1915.

GWHF15_112. Some of the ordnance dropped by LZ 77 on Wintry Park in Essex where the 2/3rd (South Midland) Field Artillery Brigade were camped with their entire ammunition supply with them. Fortunately, the bombs, though dropped accurately, failed to explode.

GWHF15_117. The Zeppelin raid on 8 September caused severe damage to Bartholomew Close, near the church of St Bartholomew the Great, and the surrounding area.

GWHF15_120. Some of the damage caused to London sub[...] during the air raid on 18 Octob[...]

GWHF15_115. During a Zeppelin raid on Paris during the night of 21 March only three bombs fell in the city. The remainder hit the suburbs of Neuilly, Courbevoie, Levallois and Asnières. The photographs show: (1) A bomb-hole in an aviation factory at Asnières; (2 and 4) A damaged building at Levallois; (3) A wrecked bedroom where two people were sleeping.

Section 4
Propaganda

GWHF15_127. On the Eastern Front, civilians died at the hands of the enemy. This photo was taken on 19 March in Memel after the Russians had left and shows the murdered sixty-three year-old landowner Michel Kurmis. Note his right hand has been hacked off.

GWHF15_128. Taken a few days later this shows Michel Kurmis' murdered staff.

GWHF15_131. Although the Battle of Loos was not the victory that was promised, it did have a propaganda value. Some of the 1,100 POWs captured during the fighting are seen being marched through the streets of Southampton.

GWHF15_134. Heroes were used for propaganda purposes. This is Sub-Lieutenant R Warneford, who was awarded the VC for destroying a Zeppelin over Belgium. He died a month later after a flying accident.

GWHF15_132. An early propaganda victory was the sinking of the German armoured cruiser Blücher on 24 January in the Dogger Bank battle. Here some of the recued sailors from the ship are being escorted to their transport before going on to a POW camp.

GWHF15_137. Counter-propaganda was designed to point the untruths of enemy propaganda to neutral and allied countries. Britain was attempting to blockade German imports by stopping ships thought to be going to Germany. This was to stop essential materials getting through and shorten the war. A photo of two portly Landsturm soldiers denying a shortage of food in Germany. 'What? And will England starve us? Oh no!'

Was? Uns will England aushungern lassen? Ach nee!

GWHF15_138. A German meat processing plant to counter Allied propaganda about food shortages.

GWHF15_139. German warehouses bursting with grain to show there was no shortage. However, there was bread rationing and soon other foods were rationed.

GWHF15_140. British counter-propaganda show the Home Front how badly off the German population were. This baker is holding German 'War Bread' which was very dark in colour and contained ingredients other than wheat, like potato flour. This is nicely contrasted with the white flour used in British bread.

Phot. Gottheil & Sohn.
Oberst v. Kurnatowski.

Hofphot.
Rumbler-Reinhard.
Oberst Tscheuschner.

Oberstleutnant Wendt.

Phot. Lindacher.
Major Ritter v. Roser.

Major v. d. Hardt.

Phot. R. Dührkoop.
Hauptmann d. R. Max Stämmler.

Phot. A. Wertheim.
Hauptmann Prestien.

Hauptmann Rasina.

Hauptmann Paul Draudt.

Hauptmann Fritz Lange.

Hofphot. Naumann Nachf.
Oberleutnant Ebert.

Phot.
Gebr. Gebauer.
Leutnant Otto Wilhelmy.

Hofphot. Benfemann.
Leutnant Robeling.

Hofphot.
Noad.
Leutnant Karl v. Scheele.

Phot.
Becker & Maaß.
Leutnant Paul Wegener.

Unteroffizier Ulli.

Inhaber des Eisernen Kreuzes I. Klasse.

GWHF15_141. Both sides published photos of heroes. This is a selection of Iron Cross First Class winners. Apart from one, they all officers.

GWHF15_142. Whilst convalescing at No. 3 Base Hospital, Sheffield, Corporal Fuller VC, of the Grenadier Guards, was presented with the Cross of the Order of St. George (third class). This had been conferred upon him by the Czar.

GWHF15_144. Captured enemy materiel on display was good for morale. Here a German aeroplane is being set up on Horse Guards Parade.

GWHF15_145. A captured German torpedo on display after it had been disarmed.

GWHF15_147. An Austrian field gun on display in a Russian city as evidence of the prowess of the Russian Army.

GWHF15_148. German artillery and a planes, captured by the French during the battles in Champagne and Artois, on display at Les Invalides. The caption wonders why this was not being done in Britain as it would surely help stimulate recruiting.

GWHF15_152. The 'murderous Triple Alliance'. A scene from a demonstration by 20,000 people in Milan urging Italy to intervene in the war on the Allied side.

GWHF15_153. A pro-intervention demonstration outside Milan Cathedral.

Section 5
Refugees and occupation

GWHF15_154. Huge numbers of refugees were housed in a huge dormitory at Alexandra Palace.

GWHF15_155. Some Belgians managed to escape by barge across the North Sea. A barge provided suitable living accommodation for more than one family.

GWHF15_156. Those who could not flee were short of food and without American aid, many would have perished. People queuing at communal soup kitchen for hot food to take home.

GWHF15_160. A soup kitchen in Belgium set up for children only.

GWHF15_163. In Berlin, East Prussian refugees were in a similar situation to the Belgians. Here they are being given clothing.

GWHF15_161. American provisions were also available for purchase by Belgian civilians who could afford them.

GWHF15_164. The Turkish massacres of Armenians increased the number of refugees in the Middle East. These Armenian children, rescued from Turkey are in a camp in Alexandria, Egypt.

GWHF15_165. Many had been saved by the French navy. Here they are resting on board a French ship and drying their clothes.

GWHF15_167. Those who stayed behind in the occupied territories had to be registered. Here the population of a French village is being photographed in groups of ten.

rückbeförderung franz. Einwohner durch die Schweiz nach Frankreich.

GWHF15_168. A French family from the occupied zone being sent to the unoccupied part of the country through Switzerland.

GWHF15_171. Not everyone was as lucky as the French family in picture 168. Some tried to escape but failed. This man was electrocuted crossing the fence between Belgium and Holland.

GWHF15_173. With a shortage of manpower women were obliged to do manual labour. Here women, under German guard, work as labourers at the Marie-Bascoun coal mines.

GWHF15_174. The manpower situation was the same in the east. Here Polish women and girls are, according to the German caption, constructing a field railway.

GWHF15_177. Prisoners were also a source of labour. These Belgian or French men, imprisoned for minor offences, are employed in road-making.

GWHF15_179. A photo to counter Allied propaganda depicting Germans as uncaring barbarians. A corporal of *63 Infantry Regiment* is holding a young child who has suffered a nappy leakage on his leg.

Another attemp
show how well
occupied and oc
got on. The own
the house and h
children listen t
played by the m
billeted on them

GWHF15_182. An early morning parade on the Grand Place in Lille to impress on the inhabitants the might of Germany.

GWHF15_185.
While many Belgians in the cities were starving, farmers sold their surplus freely. Here men from the front are buying provisions to take back with them.

GWHF15_186. With school teachers in the army, schools were staffed by Germans. This is a German-French war school in the Champagne region.

GWHF15_193. Serbs of military age being marched off to internment.

GWHF15_189. Bread was scarce across the fighting zone. Here Polish civilians are queuing for their bread ration.

GWHF15_187. Eve[n] children were likely t[o] stopped and searche[d] photo, taken near the border, shows a guar[d] checking the children['s] basket for contraban[d]

GWHF15_188. The German Army became the law. It regularly convened courts, often trivial matters.

Section 6
Casualties

GWHF15_195. Lists were very important in wartime. This is the casualty bureau in Berlin where people were employed making lists of those wounded.

GWHF15_194. Many towns and villages created a Roll of Honour when the first men volunteered. These became Rolls of Remembrance for those who fell. This is the Chew Magna roll which, by early 1915, was running out of space.

GWHF15_200. Wounded soldier and sailors usually returned to Bri on converted hospital ships. This yacht, the *Catania*, was given by th Duke of Sutherland as a temporary hospital before it became an armed steam yacht in the Mediterranean.

GWHF15_203. To train the regular influx of new men into the VAD, and to make the transfer of wounded as smooth as possible, it was necessary to rehearse between busy periods.

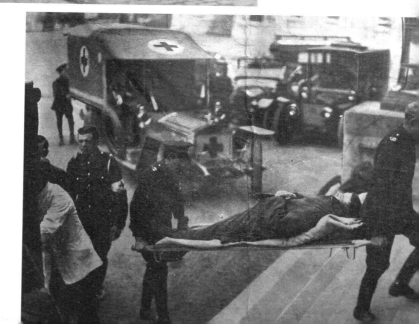

GWHF15_204. Arrival of the wounded at the hospital. As the times of the trains carrying the wounded were known in advance, it was possible to be ready for their arrival.

Examination Schools, Oxford, now 3rd Southern General Hospital.

GWHF15_206. Many large public buildings were taken over as casualties mounted. This is the Examination Schools building on High Street, Oxford. It had 346 beds, including 94 beds for orthopaedic cases and 25 for what were described as 'nerve cases'.

READING WAR HOSPITAL.

GWHF15_205. Reading War Hospital began its life in 1867 as a workhouse, the Reading Union Workhouse, and between 1889 and 1892 an infirmary was added with 185 beds for vagrants. In 1915 it was taken over by the War Office and converted into a major military hospital. In 1930 it became Battle Hospital. In order to make the wounded men more comfortable, a War Hospital Care and Comforts Committee was set up to provide clothing, books, tobacco and many other items.

WHF15_209. The Czar provided the wounded with a palace for convalescence. This is the ...nter Palace at Petrograd, ...sibly the most magnificent ...l luxurious hospital ward ...ing the war. It was known ...Tsarevitch Alexis Hospital ...er his son.

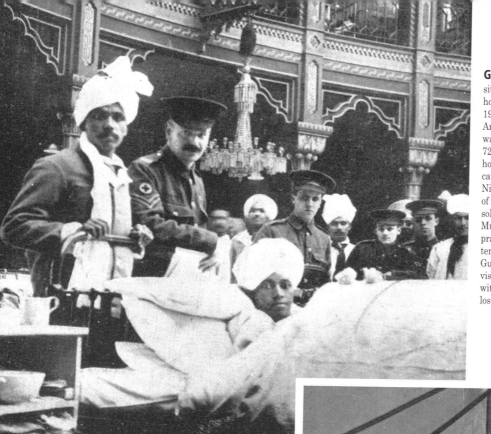

GWHF15_210. The Pavilion, along with o[ther] sites in Brighton, was transformed into a mi[litary] hospital. Between December 1914 and Janua[ry] 1916, sick and wounded soldiers from the In[dian] Army were treated in the former royal palac[e. It] was set up with two operating theatres and c[...] 720 beds. Over 2,300 men were treated at th[e] hospital. Elaborate arrangements were mad[e to] cater for the patients' religious and cultural [...] Nine different kitchens were set up in the gr[ounds] of the hospital, so that food could be cooked b[y the] soldiers' fellow caste members and co-religio[nists.] Muslims were given space on the eastern law[n to] pray to Mecca, while Sikhs were provided wit[h a] tented gurdwara in the grounds. Pictured is a[...] Gurkha soldier, Bal, who had lost a leg. On h[is] visit to the hospital on 9 January, the King ta[lked] with this soldier. His brother in a bed nearby [had] lost an arm.

GWHF15_211. A common scene in hospital in Britain.

GWHF15_212. A similar picture taken in a German hospital.

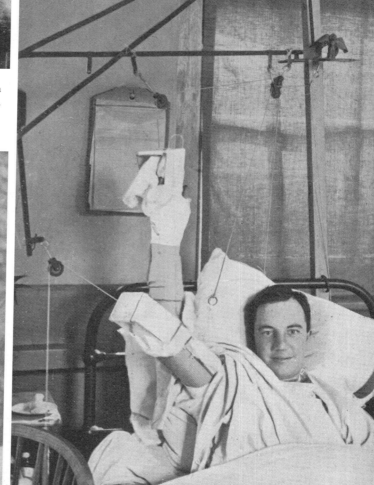

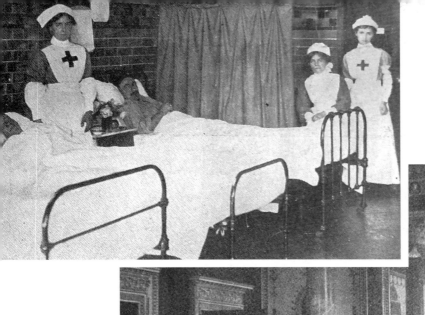

GWHF15_213. A few were lucky and convalesced in luxurious surroundings, but for the majority any warm secure building stood in as a hospital. This typical makeshift ward is in the Church House of All Saints', Wokingham, then an auxiliary of Reading War Hospital.

HF15_214. Members e Guards Brigade were cared for at Basildon . These guardsmen are ng in the Dante room.

HF15_215. A large building in Germany erted into a large tal for convalescents.

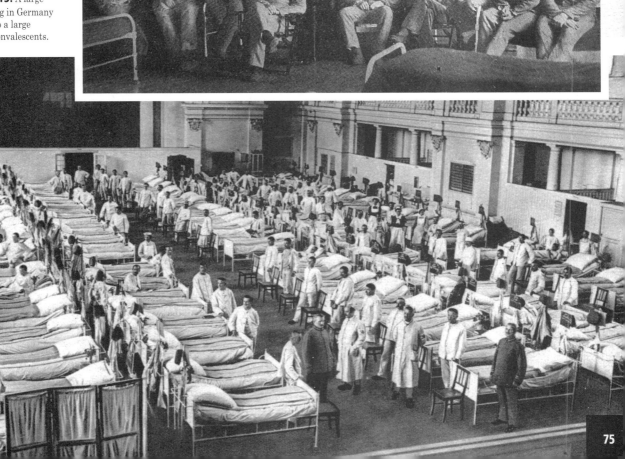

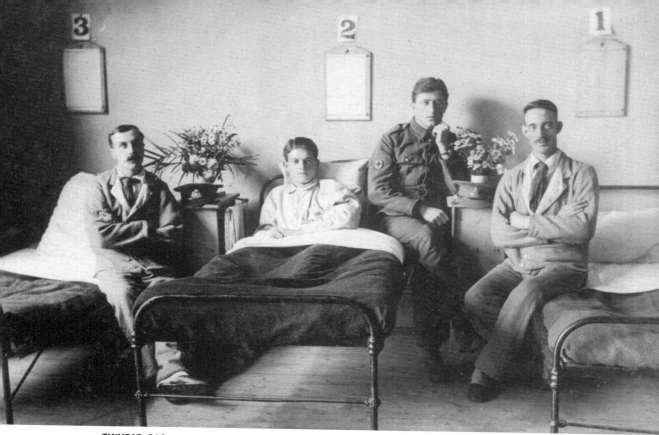

GWHF15_216. Private Terry with three convalescents in a small hospital in Hastings.

GWHF15_217. A small convalescent hospital in Germany. Note one of the men has a bottle of spirits with him: that would not be allowed in a British hospital.

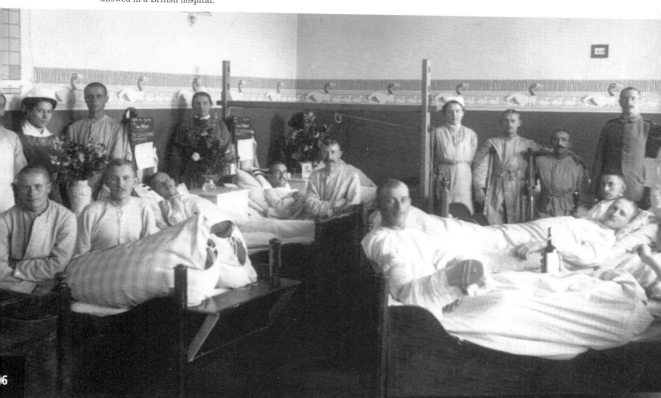

GWHF15_218. Off-duty hours in Duffield War Hospital near Derby. On the wall is the town's Roll of Honour.

GWHF15_219. To alleviate boredom in the hospitals, groups were formed to provide visitors and entertainment. This could range from a musical recital, as shown here, or a large group of entertainers providing concerts.

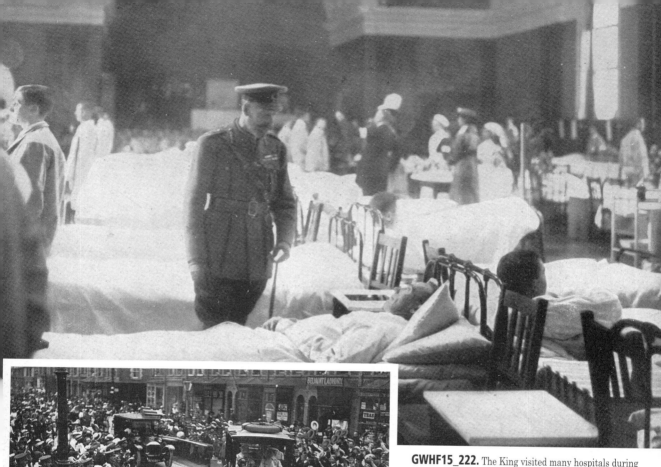

GWHF15_222. The King visited many hospitals during the war. This one was in Torquay.

GWHF15_221. Royal visits always cause a big crowd. This is the arrival of the King and Queen to the newly opened Reading War Hospital.

GWHF15_220. A famous Russian opera singer, Shaliapine, opened his own hospital in Moscow. Here he is seen entertaining some of the wounded.

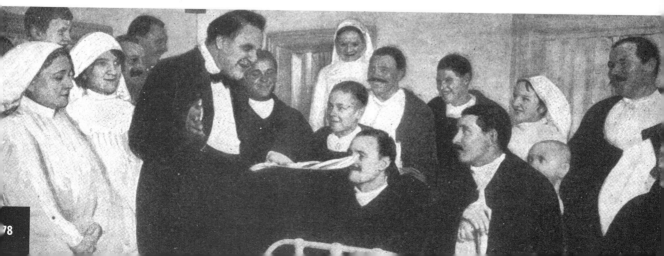

GWHF15_224. Not only in Britain did royalty visit the wounded. This shows Archduchess Zita, wife of the heir to the Austrian throne, on the roof-garden of a hospital in Vienna.

GWHF15_225. In Berlin, wounded soldiers are visited by Princess August Wilhelm.

GWHF15_229. Princess Hildegard of Bavaria (marked with a x) was a nurse in a Munich hospital.

GWHF15_228. Princess Henry of Pless working as a nurse in a Berlin hospital. British by birth she was married to a German noble.

GWHF15_226. A scene on a ward in the hospital at Tsarköe Selo during a visit by the Russian Empress.

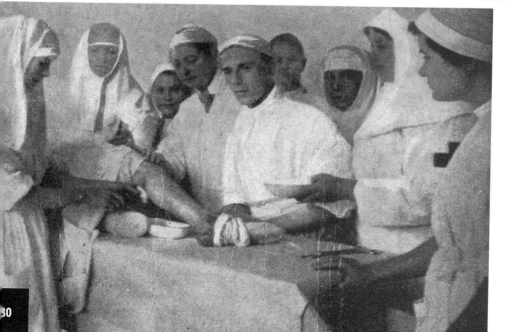

GWHF15_227. Royalty at work. Here, the Grand Duchess Tatiana tends the wounds of a Russian soldier.

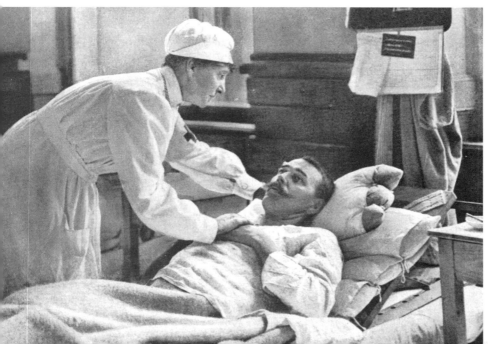

GWHF15_230. In the centre of the photo is the Grand Duchess Marie, wife of the Grand Duke George Mikhailovitch, cousin of the Tsar, and sister of the King of Greece. Stranded in Britain by the war, she opened a small hospital in Harrogate. This grew from twelve to fifty beds. On the left of the Grand Duchess is Princess Margaret of Denmark.

GWHF15_231. The Austrian Archduchess Maria, wife of Archduke Charles, known as Sister Michaela, helping a wounded soldier.

GWHF15_232. To prevent boredom and assist recovery, the wounded were sometimes taken out into the countryside by those who could afford a car. These soldiers are being transported in Humber cars, provided by the company for the wounded in Coventry hospitals.

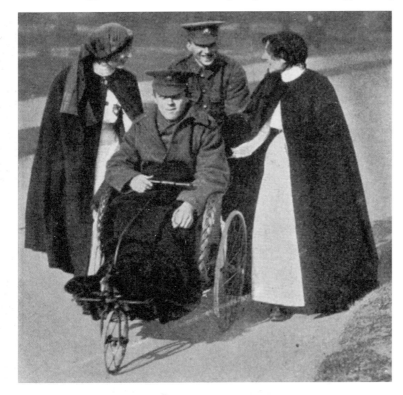

GWHF15_233. At any time of year, whenever the weather was suitable, men were taken outside to benefit from sunlight.

GWHF15_234. In towns and cities with rivers, boat rides were very popular. This is the MV Alexandra on the Thames

GWHF15_235. Princess Alexandra leaving Marlborough House to the cheers of a group of convalescent soldiers enjoying a constitutional.

GWHF15_236. King George frequently put his carriages at the disposal of the war hospital. In Berlin, and Potsdam, the Kaiser did the same. In the latter, the convalescents were taken through the Park of his summer residence, Sans Souci.

GWHF15_239. By 1915 wounded soldiers were a common sight. For the seriously injured, classes were provided to help them integrate into civilian life. Here a female teacher instructs men to write with the left hand.

GWHF15_240. St. Dunstan's was created in 1915 to help servicemen who had suffered sight loss. One of its purposes was to train them for employment. Basket making was one trade taught.

GWHF15_241. Roehampton House, one of Queen Mary's Convalescent Auxiliary Hospitals, specialised in caring for men who had lost limbs. Up to 275 could be treated at a time.

GWHF15_242. A double amputee being taught a skill in a German hospital.

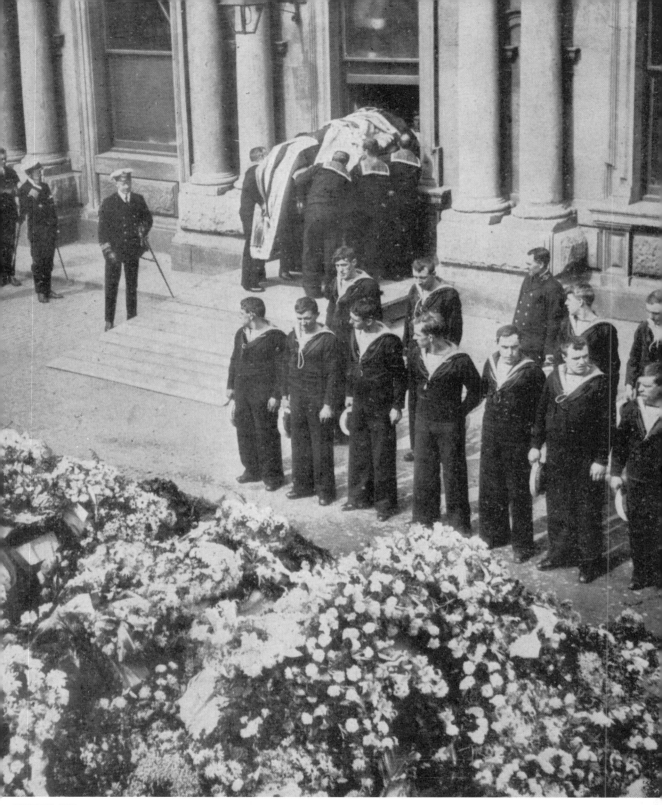

GWHF15_243. On 18 August, submarine E13 ran aground in Danish waters. Despite violating Denmark's neutrality, two German torpedo boats fired on the submarine from a distance of 300 yards, damaging the vessel and killing fifteen men. Their bodies were taken aboard a Danish vessel to Hull before being taken to their respective home towns for burial. This shows the coffins arriving at Hull Paragon station.

GWHF15_246. The coffins containing the dead from the E13 being escorted through Hull on their way to the station.

GWHF15_248. Only days after destroying a Zeppelin and being awarded the VC, Sub-Lieutenant Warneford died in a flying accident in France. His passenger, Henry Needham, was killed in the crash. Warneford died on the way to hospital.

GWHF15_249. The burial of Warneford VC in Brompton Cemetery on 22 June was attended by 50,000 spectators. Men of the Royal Naval Division provided the firing and bugle parties.

GWHF15_250. Many famous sportsmen had rallied to the call and some paid the ultimate price. A major loss to the rowing fraternity was Ralph Le Blanc-Smith, a Cambridge oarsman. He joined the navy at the start of the war but transferred to the Rifle Brigade with a commission. He was killed on 27 November.

SEC·LIEUT THE HON. CHARLES T. MILLS, M.P.
(SCOTS GUARDS.)

CAPT THE HON. A.E.B. O'NEILL, M.P.
(2nd. LIFE GUARDS.)

LORD NINIAN CRICHTON-STUART, M.P.
(6th BATTN WELSH REGIMENT.)

CAPT HAROLD T. CAWLEY, M.P.
(MANCHESTER REGIMENT.)

CAPT W. G. C. GLADSTONE, M.P.
(R. WELSH FUSILIERS)

LIEUT THE HON. T.C.R. AGAR-ROBARTES, M.P.
(R. BUCKS HUSSARS YEOMANRY.)

GWHF15_251. Many MPs had also gone to the front. These six, 'young men of high promise', were killed.

GWHF15_253. General von Emmich, victor of the Battle of Liège, died on 22 December in Hannover. He was given a state funeral.

GWHF15_254. Captain Erdmann, commander of the Blücher, which took part in the raid on Scarborough and was sunk in the Dogger Bank battle, died in captivity on 16 February. He was buried with full military honours on 18 February in Edinburgh. There was considerable controversy at the time about whether someone who had been involved in the Scarborough raid should have received such an honour.

GWHF15_256. In France, women in mourning visited the graves of British soldiers. This may have been some small consolation for those bereaved.

GWHF15_257. Indian soldiers who died in Britain could not be buried for religious reasons. Arrangements were made for open-air cremations: an unusual sight in England.

Zum frommen Andenken im Gebete
an den tugendsamen Jüngling

Johann Mühlbauer,

Oederterbauersjohn von Wald,
Pfarrei Wang,

Soldat beim k. bay. 12. Inf.-Reg. 11. Komp
welcher am 11. Dezember 1915 im Alter
von 20 Jahren bei Cheeville in Frankreich
den Heldentod fürs Vaterland starb.

Schwer hat uns der Schlag getroffen,
Doch er kam von Gottes Hand,
Der geliebte Sohn und Bruder
Starb den Tod fürs Vaterland

Vater unser   Ave Maria.

Druck von Hans Grau in Wasserburg.

Zur frommen Erinnerung
im Gebete an den tugendsamen Jüngling

Josef Birnbeck

von Rosenheim

Kriegsfreiwilliger im 249. Infant.-Regiment,
7. Kompagnie

welche am 7. August 1915 in Russland im
Alter von 18½ Jahren den Heldentod fürs
Vaterland gestorben ist.

O Herr, gib ihm die ewige Ruhe!

Auf Wiedersehn! Dein letztes Wort
Beim Waffenaufgebot;
Auf Wiedersehn! So klang es fort
Trotz Schlacht- und Todesnot.
Auf Wiedersehn! Dein letztes Wort,
Ich schreib es auf dein Grab;
Auf Wiedersehn im Himmel dort,
Senkt man uns einst hinab.
                M. Niedermayr Rosenheim.

Christliches Andenken
in Gebete
an den ehrengeachteten Jüngling

Franz Wengbauer

Walzingerjohn von Simmling, zuletzt
Oekonomie-Baumeister in Laufen

Soldat bei der k. u. k. Armee,
gestorben im Kriegsgefangenenspital zu
Nikolsk im 41. Lebensjahre für Kaiser
und Vaterland am 16. Dezember 1915.

Es senkt des Todes dunkle Nacht
Sich auf ein arbeitsfreudig Leben,
Er hat vollendet, hat's vollbracht
In kühnem Vorwärtsstreben.
Man hat den tapfern Heldenleib
Begraben im fremden Land,
Gott führ ihn auf ins ew'ge Licht
Mit gütig-milder Hand.

Buchdruckerei A. Huber, Kittmoning.

GWHF15_259. Common among Catholic families in Europe was the death picture. This is for Austrian Franz Wengbauer who died in hospital on 16 December.

GWHF15_260. Many younger men did not wait to be called up. War Volunteer Josef Birnbeck was just eighteen and a half when he was killed in Russia.

GWHF15_261. Better-off families could afford to have a real photo attached the death card that was given to friends and relatives. Johann Mühlhauser, a Bavarian soldier, was killed on 11 December in France.

GWHF15_262. Less common in Britain: a photographic memorial card for a British sailor.

In Loving Memory.

Private JOHN ALEXANDER GRAHAM,
Aged 23 years;

KILLED IN THE DARDANELLES ON MAY 31, 1915,
WHEN CONVEYING RATIONS TO THE
FIRING LINE.

*"Greater love hath no man than this : that a
man lay down his life for his friends."*

GWHF15_263. The opening of a new front in the Dardanelles meant more casualties. A printed British death card for Private Graham of the 1st/7th Manchester Regiment.

GWHF15_266. Not all the casualties were young men. This is the death card for forty-year-old Sergeant Venn, a married man from Willington.

GWHF15_269. 'At 6.49 am on Saturday 22 May 1915 a Liverpool-bound troop-train carrying half (498 all ranks) of the 7th (Leith) Battalion, The Royal Scots... collided head on with a local passenger train, which had been 'parked', facing north, on the south-bound main line at Quintinshill, just North of Gretna, to allow a following express to overtake it...The troop train overturned, mostly onto the neighbouring north-bound mainline track and, a minute later, the Glasgow-bound express ploughed into the wreckage causing it to burst into flame. The ferocity of the fire, and consequent difficulty of rescuing those trapped in the overturned and mangled carriages, was compounded by the fact that most of the carriages were very old, made of wood and lit by gas contained in a tank beneath them. Between the crash and the fire a total of 216 all ranks of 7RS and 12 others, ...mostly from the express but including the driver and fireman on the troop-train, died in, or as an immediate result of what was, and remains, Britain's worst railway disaster.' This is a temporary hospital in a field near the line.

GWHF15_270. Survivors of the train crash at roll call.

GWHF15_271/271a. The burning carriage in which some of the men perished. Only the metal frame was left.

GWHF15_272. Nurse Edith Cavell was executed by the Germans on 12 October for helping Allied soldiers escape to Holland.

Section 7
Wartime life

GWHF15_274. Colonel Cochrane presenting the Women's Reserve Ambulance Corps with colours.

GWHF15_275. The staff at the 'Snapshots from Home League' office, dealing with applications. They sent any soldier at the front a photograph of anyone, or a view from home.

GWHF15_276. Men and women in a technical class together learning the basics of machine tool work.

GWHF15_277. Mrs Pankhurst addressing a meeting at the London Pavilion on war service for women. With the advent of the War, she and her eldest daughter Christabel called an immediate halt to militant suffrage activism in support of the government. They urged women to aid industrial production and encouraged young men to fight, becoming prominent figures in the white feather movement.

GWHF15_278. In July, organised by Emmeline Pankhurst, there was a demonstration in London, when women marched demanding the 'Right to Serve'.

GWHF15_280. With increased numbers of women in employment, there was an increase in the number of day nurseries, which again increased the number of working women.

GWHF15_281. Day nurseries then did not have to pass today's rigorous inspection standards - as can be seen in this photo. In this nursery between eighteen and twenty children were cared for on a daily basis while their mothers were at work.

GWHF15_285. Women of all combatant nations made articles fo their troops. These are Bavarian co ladies working in the King of Bavaria's Palace in Munich.

GWHF15_282. Increased numbers of POWs meant that more parcels, containing necessities not provided by the Germans, needed to be sent abroad. Women volunteers packed parcels at depots across the country. This is a warehouse at St. John's Gate.

GWHF15_283. Wages increased, but not to the benefit of everyone. There were still poor who could not afford the rising prices. This photo was taken in East London where local suffragettes provided the poor with a lunch for twopence.

GWHF15_289. Women making articles for wives of soldiers at the front at the Hammersmith branch of the "Tipperary Homes".

GWHF15_287. An eighty-seven year-old woman in Germany knitting for the troops.

GWHF15_290. Children also became involved in the mass production of articles for men at the front. These are the Guild of Brave Poor Things, girls and women who were either blind or disabled in some way.

GWHF15_286. A similar scene in Russia. These are noblewomen from Petrograd working to make bandages and respirators.

GWHF15_294. Volunteers dealing with gas pads.

GWHF15_296. Before the war, Germany had been the major source of lenses for optical equipment. With this source cut off, British firms were obliged to make them to the same quality. These women are being trained in lens making at the Northampton Institute.

GWHF15_293. A party from the George Palmer Girls' School in Reading who started war work in the autumn of 1915. They made pyjamas, bed-jackets and padded wire splints.

GWHF15_295. Volunteers making gas pads.

GWHF15_297. A simple way of telling whether a shell casting was faulty was to hit it with a hammer and listen to the sound. This is a French shell manufacturing plant.

GWHF15_298. With the rapid call-up in France, women quickly replaced men in many jobs. These women workers, employed in the Schneider workshops in Chalon-sur-Saone, are checking sizes and making shell fuses.

GWHF15_299. A similar scene in a British munitions plant.

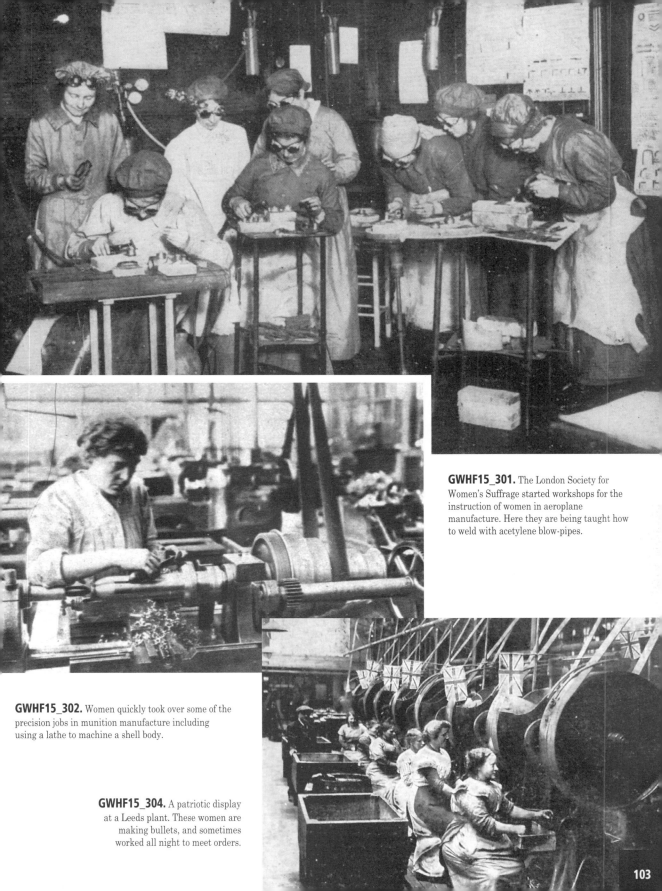

GWHF15_301. The London Society for Women's Suffrage started workshops for the instruction of women in aeroplane manufacture. Here they are being taught how to weld with acetylene blow-pipes.

GWHF15_302. Women quickly took over some of the precision jobs in munition manufacture including using a lathe to machine a shell body.

GWHF15_304. A patriotic display at a Leeds plant. These women are making bullets, and sometimes worked all night to meet orders.

GWHF15_307. Barges would traditionally be towed by horses or men. With the army requisitioning many horses, and the men joining the colours, this work was left to women. Here, mother and daughter are seen towing a barge along Regent's Canal.

GWHF15_306. Two female chimney sweeps, mother and daughter, in Germany.

GWHF15_305. As well as taking employment in munitions, women took over many other traditionally male jobs. Here, making domestic gas, are Mrs Summers and her daughter at work at Chew Magna near Bristol. They made the gas for the village under the supervision of a male manager.

GWHF15_308. Two women dispatch riders on official business free two more men for the front.

GWHF15_309. Another traditionally all-male environment was the smithy. Here Mrs Saunders, of Aldbro Hatch in Essex, is being instructed by her husband. She has replaced her two sons, one of whom had been killed in the Dardanelles.

GWHF15_311. There was opposition to women police but they quickly became a common sight. Here one is guarding works of art in an exhibition and the photo underneath shows a female member of the force in Bow Street, London.

GWHF15_310. Women unloading a coal wagon – another previously all-male domain.

GWHF15_315. After initial opposition, Reading Council followed other councils in employing women on the trams. These are the first of Reading Tramway's female conductresses.

GWHF15_314. Inspecting tickets at a main line station.

GWHF15_317. Even with a war on, there was still a need for railway porters. Men were replaced by women and boys.

GWHF15_318. A female postal worker in Dresden. Every country fighting had the same shortage of men, but no shortage of women happy to take their place.

Posthalterei Dresden.

GWHF15_319. Russia was very quick to make use of women and in 1914 was employing them as drivers on trams. This picture shows two female tramway employees, a driver and conductress.

GWHF15_322. In order to allow munitions workers some time off, more prosperous men, and some women, took shifts at the weekend. Upwards of 10,000 London professional and business men enrolled in the Volunteer Munitions Brigade by the end of 1915. Here they are shown at lunch-time.

GWHF15_324. To protect their surfaces from knocks which might make them impossible to fire, shells were transported in wicker covers.

GWHF15_326. Shells manufactured in Sheffield stacked ready for dispatch to explosive filling plants.

GWHF15_327. A similar pile of shells, but larger calibre, waiting for despatch from a French plant.

GWHF15_329. In 1915 there was no conscription, so many skilled men continued in their peace-time occupations as lathe workers, but now making munitions. By the end of the war, most of them would be in the army while women replaced them in their jobs.

NO TREATING

Under the Defence of the Realm Act Every person must pay for their own drink at the time of ordering.

GWHF15_335. The sign that suddenly appeared in every bar across the country. It was meant to be a positive act but it was not popular with many drinkers.

GWHF15_340. An alleged German spy caught on a ship in Dunkirk harbour and arrested on the point of embarking for England.

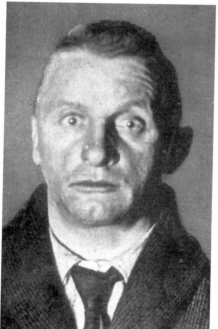

GWHF15_339. Although the government had dealt with the spy problem in 1914, there were regular scares like this one: a harmless clergyman, the Reverend Siviter, on holiday with a pair of binoculars. Someone's healthy imagination added a sketch pad and mused on him sitting on the Isle of Wight watching and drawing. After thirty minutes of questioning, he was able to prove he was the new curate at Totland Bay and allowed to go.

GWHF15_338. Werner von Horn, an officer in the reserve, could not return to Germany from Guatemala because of the British blockade and became a saboteur. In February he attempted to blow up the Vanceboro bridge across the St. Croix River between New Brunswick and Maine. He was indicted and jailed in America for eighteen months. On release he was extradited to Canada where he was again jailed but released in 1921, when he was certified insane, and sent back to Germany.

GWHF15_337. To counteract the reduced lighting, many areas painted bases of lamp posts white and marked trees in a similar fashion. This is a tree in Acton being passed by a 1915 model Talbot. Car manufacturers designed a new style for each year.

GWHF15_341. The spy was a world-wide menace. This is a German spy, found on the docks at Montreal, being escorted to a military prison.

FOR OUR BRAVE BOYS

FOR OUR WOUNDED HEROES.

GWHF15_342. A national collection that did not always take money, although it did if offered, was the egg fund for wounded sailors and soldiers. This is a display of eggs collected by a non-conformist church for the local hospital.

GWHF15_344. The rich could afford to give a little more. This is an auction of art and other collectables given to raise funds for the National Relief Fund.

GWHF15_346. Pets were a good way to collect money. This is Mrs Ashford Green's collie, Laddie, who raised £3 10s 1d for the Russian Red Cross and in 1915 £15 for the Prince of Wales' Fund.

GWHF15_345. By 1915 the flag day had become a regular occurrence with money being raised for many charities. The slow speed of vehicles in towns made it easy to stop the traffic and sell flags.

GWHF15_348. All types of people helped sell flags but only in Italy did royalty join in. This is the Prince of Piedmont, heir to the throne and only son of the King of Italy, who was selling Red Cross postcards in the Quirinal – a Royal Palace in Rome – attended by a guard of Boy Scouts.

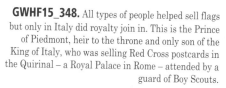

GWHF15_349. A lethal combination – children and an animal collecting for Belgium. Later in the war, such young children had to be with an adult if they were collecting.

GWHF15_350. A very young Red Cross nurse pinning a flag on a soldier during Wounded Soldiers' Day.

GWHF15_351. A giant statue of Hindenburg built out of wood. For a Mark, the giver could hammer a nail into the statue. Money raised in this way went to war charities in Germany.

GWHF15_352. Hammering nails into statues caught on as a way of fund-raising. This is Captain von Müller of the cruiser Emden – a national hero – portrayed as a mail-clad knight.

GWHF15_354. Most flags sold in Britain were small and made of paper. This is a flag seller in Berlin who is selling full-sized flags.

GWHF15_355. To help alleviate shortages both si[de]s introduced national collect[ion] to recycle materials. These people are sorting through garments collected during Reichs Wool Week.

GWHF15_356. German schoolboys during Wool Week taking their reclaimed articles to the central collection depot.

GWHF15_358. In Germany the rich gave gold and other precious items to be sold to finance the war.

GWHF15_357. With no access to copper ore because of the British blockade Germany had to find supplies from somewhere. Recycling was the obvious answer. Here children in school add their family's contribution to the national copper collection.

GWHF15_362. Although everyone backed the fight against Germany, there were still sectional interests, particularly when it was seen that some employers were making profits that did not benefit their workforce, or when male status in the workplace was threatened. This is Lloyd George addressing the South Wales miners during a dispute in July.

GWHF15_361. Lloyd George addressing the crowd at the Women's Right to Serve march in July. He wanted as many women as possible to come forward to work in munitions.

GWHF15_364. The Clyde, a shipbuilding centre, was another area that was affected by industrial action. No le[ss] patriotic than other parts of the country, Clyde-side workers were more militant and had strong socialist beliefs.

GWHF15_369. Many men who were too old to enlist became Special Constables. As a group, they inspired little confidence in the public and were the butt of many local and national jokes.

COMPANY-SERGT.-MAJOR HARRY DANIELS, V.C.

PRIVATE WILLIAM BUCKINGHAM, V.C.

THE LATE PRIVATE JACOB RIVERS, V.C.

THE LATE ACTING-CORPORAL CECIL REGINALD NOBLE, V.C.

GWHF15_367. Early in the morning of 1 January 1915, in heavy seas, HMS *Formidable* sank after being hit by two torpedoes. Captain William Pillar and the crew of the trawler *Provident* rescued 72 officers and men from the ship. For his work Pillar was decorated by the King with the Distinguished Service Medal.

GWHF15_368. Stories of Victoria Cross winners helped to give the impression that everything was going well and that the army was doing well.

GWHF15_370. Although German propaganda photos aimed to show that there was plenty of food available, this is a food queue in Berlin where meat and other necessities were distributed to the poor.

GWHF15_373. There were many ways to help the war effort. These are Eton schoolboys helping load limbers and guns during the weekend.

GWHF15_374. Some British schoolboys joined the OTC or cadets. In Germany the same age group became 'Boy Recruits' and trained at army camps to become soldiers.

GWHF15_375. Some German cities ran paramilitary youth organisations. These are pre-military age youths from Dresden on a route march.

GWHF15_378. To make sure that docks ran smoothly a number of Dockers Battalions were formed to deal with cargo. Men enlisted into the Transport Workers' Battalions were guaranteed no overseas service in return for their following orders if there were issues with other employees on the docks.

GWHF15_380. Rising costs and increasing shortages of some foodstuffs resulted in the same solution on both sides: grow your own. Many people who had no previous experience of gardening took an allotment to supplement their food supply. This is a mass allotment in Germany being tended by school children.

GWHF15_381. The land needed lookin after and, as men were in short supply, women and children took their place. Thi Lady Petre, in mourning for her husband Lieutenant Lord Petre who had fallen in action, with some of the pupils of her dair farm at Thorndon Hall in Essex. They proved to be an admirable substitute for farm-hands on active service.

GWHF15_383. There were insufficient farm hands to bring in the 1915 harvest, s the army released a number of men to hel This was not always successful as those men who were released often lacked experience of the land.

GWHF15_384. The same solution was applied in France where soldiers helped farmers' wives to bring in the crops.

GWHF15_385. Another answer to the shortage of men was using convalescent soldiers. These are wounded Australians helping bring in the harvest in a Surrey village.

GWHF15_386. Before the introduction of the Women's Auxiliary Army Corps, the army employed female labour whenever possible. This is the central forage depot where at least half the workers are female.

GWHF15_389. Crowds gathered to celebrate Italy's entry into the war on the Allied side. On the balcony are King Victor, Queen Helen and the Royal Family.

GWHF15_392. The firs[t] anniversary of the war w[as] marked across the countr[y with] religious services and processions. This is the G[reat] War 'Dad's Army', march[ing] along Broad Street in Rea[ding.]

GWHF15_391. Demon[strations] in Bucharest in favour of [the] Entente Powers had to be controlled by the army. A majority wanted to join t[he war] against Germany, but the [King] and most ministers prefe[rred to] stay neutral.

GWHF15_393. A public demonstration following the Russian naval victory at Riga Bay. A large crowd assembled outside the Russian Embassy to cheer the Tsar and the King. A military band played the British and Russian anthems to close the proceedings. The Russian Ambassador, Count Benckendorff, appeared on one of the balconies to express his appreciation of the sympathy and friendship displayed.

GWHF15_394. A similar scene in Berlin following the conquest of Warsaw.

GWHF15_395. A large crowd gathered at the Bismarck memorial on 1 April to celebrate the centenary of his birth. Bismarck, the first chancellor of the German Empire, was the driving force behind the unification of Germany. His diplomacy of realpolitik and powerful rule at home gained him the nickname the "Iron Chancellor". As a result he was venerated by much of the population.

GWHF15_396. The Bishop of London, Dr Ingram, preaching by a drum-altar on the steps of St. Paul's. 'It is the soul of England which is once again to free the world' was his message to the assembled troops.

GWHF15_397. General Botha's enthusiastic welcome on his return to Cape Town on 22 July after his successful campaign in German West Africa.

GWHF15_398. A huge crowd assembled to watch the Manchester Pals battalions march through the city with the salute taken by Lord Kitchener.

GWHF15_399. On the anniversary of the war, large crowds formed at important landmarks. This is outside Reading Town Hall, round Queen Victoria's statue.

GWHF15_400. Every country ran War Loans campaigns to encourage the population to inves their country, ostensibly to purchase weapons. I is the first day of a new war loan in Germany. I were exchanging gold for paper loan certificates

GWHF15_402. In the courtyard of the Bank of England, applying for a War Loan prospectus.

GWHF15_403. Many larger British companies encouraged their work force to invest in war loans and bonds, some even sharing the cost as an incentive. These are employees of Waring and Gillow being addressed by Mr Waring and and ex-employee, Sergeant Belcher VC.

GWHF15_405. Compare this photo with 400 and 402. This is the exchange of gold for paper at the Bank of France at the start of a war loan.

GWHF15_410. Millions of completed forms needed a small army of collators to check each paper and record the details.

GWHF15_406. Children were encouraged to save money and schools' savings clubs facilitated this.

GWHF15_408. The National Registration told the government the exact number of men who were eligible for military service. These officials are instructing heads of households how to fill in the forms.

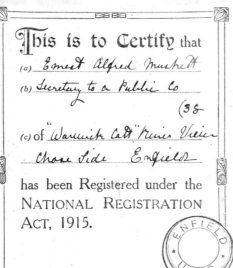

This is to Certify that

(a) *Ernest Alfred Muskett*

(b) *Secretary to a Public Co*

(38

(c) of *"Warwick Cott" River View*
Chase Side Enfield

has been Registered under the
NATIONAL REGISTRATION
ACT, 1915.

Signature
of
Holder. *R. A. Muskett*

GOD SAVE THE KING.

(a) Name.   (b) Occupation.   (c) Postal Address

GWHF15_413. The inside of the National Registration card that everyone had to carry at all times.

GWHF15_417. The King and Queen on their w the special intercessory service at St. Paul's Cath on 4 August.

GWHF15_418. The King at the memorial service for those killed at Gallipoli.

GWHF15_419. King George visited many munitions plants during the war. In July he visited the works of Messrs. Kynoch, Ltd., the Birmingham Small Arms Company's factories at Small Heath, and the wagons work at Saltley. This was taken at Kynoch's, the ammunition manufacturer.

GWHF15_420. This is a munition factory in Birmingham which the King visited.

pl. THOMAS
NE, 7th Batt.
Yorks Regt.

Corpl. JAMES H.
BYRNE, Army Ord-
nance Corps.

Miss B. A. BYRNE,
Nurse Sister in
France.

Sergt.-Major J.
BYRNE, Recruiting
Sergeant.

Miss M. E. BYRNE,
Nurse at the
Dardanelles.

Corpl. PETER A.
BYRNE, Army Ord-
nance Corps.

Bugler CHRISTO-
PHER A. BYRNE,
3/4th Batt. Royal
Berks Regiment.

Corpl. LEONARD
JOHN BYRNE, 12th
Batt. King's Royal
Rifle Corps.

GWHF15_425. Many families were able to take pride in having six family members in the forces, but few could boast of two daughters on active service. The Byrne family had six male family members in the army and two daughters serving as nurses, one in France and one at Gallipoli.

Sons of Mr. and Mrs. E. HINXMAN, 32, South St., Caversham (seven in the Army and one in the Police Force).

Pte. H. HINXMAN,
Army Service Corps.

Pte. A. W. HINX-
MAN, Royal Army
Medical Corps
(motor driver).

Pte. C. HINXMAN,
Army Service Corps,
M.T.

Pte. A. McA. HINX-
MAN, Duke of
Cornwall's Light
Infantry.—Wounded.

Pte. F. J. HINX-
MAN, Army Service
Corps, M.T.

Pte. J. F. HINX-
MAN, Duke of Corn-
wall's L.I.

Spr. R. HINXMAN,
Royal Engineers.

Police-Constable G.
HINXMAN, Metro-
politan Police.

GWHF15_426. Equalling the Byrne family, in numbers, was the Hinxman family. There were differences though, they were all sons, and did the police officer really count?

GWHF15_421. The Tsar, as well as visiting hospitals, also went to munitions plants. This is the Putiloff works at Petrograd.

GWHF15_428. As the army abroad grew in size so did the volume of mail. Each of these bags is for a different unit. The two at the front are for the 1st and 8th East Yorkshires. Behind are sacks for battalions of the Yorkshire Regiment and then the Welsh Regiment.

GWHF15_430. Not quite as organised as the British system but equally busy. A German sub-post office sorting soldiers' mail.

PARCELS TO PRISONERS OF WAR

AND THE

TROOPS AT HOME & ABROAD.

Send for Special List compiled with a view to facilitating the selection of Goods for despatch to the Expeditionary Forces in various countries, also Home Forces, and Prisoners of War.

One of the large Daily Consignments sent from our Store.

You send us the Order—We do the rest.

GREGORY, LOVE & CO., LTD.,

THE STORES, READING.

GWHF15_429. For the busy family, there were stores which took the order and then did the rest. This is a typical advert for such a company.

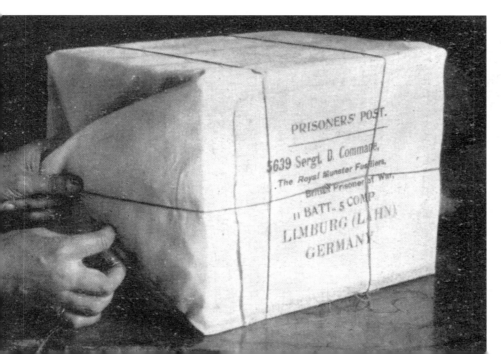

GWHF15_431. Parcels for POWs had to be a certain size and packed in a certain way. They were not handled by the Post Office but sent through the offices of the International Red Cross.

GWHF15_433. Thro
the war both sides exc
POWs. Usually they w
men who would be me
discharged because of
wounds, but these look
healthy.

GWHF15_434. Britis
exchanged POWs that a
in England, from Germ
on 7 December. Compa
these men with the Ger
exchanged POWs.

Section 8
Christmas

GWHF15_437. A formal Christmas photo, taken in a school hall converted into a War Hospital.

GWHF15_436. The second Christmas of the war – a scene inside a convalescent hospital on Christmas Day. Every effort was made by the staff to make the day enjoyable for the wounded. A bumper Christmas dinner with large quantities of food and refreshments was part of the treat.

GWHF15_448. A Home Front Christmas postcard for sending to the men at the front.

GWHF15_438. Christmas was a special time in Germany. This is the Christmas dinner given to the children of Dresden men who were at the front.

GWHF15_442. Despite the war, Christmas and the New Year were still the party season. Fancy dress for a Christmas party in Hull.

GWHF15_439. Manchester City Hall on Christmas Day. A meal was laid on for wounded men and local families. The men and women are segregated and the nurses are providing the service.

GWHF15_440. Some employers were very generous to their employees who had enlisted. Here is a pile of presents for Humber Limited servicemen. Each parcel contained a pipe, tobacco, cigarettes, a Christmas pudding, potted meat, a muffler, and other gifts.

CHRISTMAS, 1915.

To *Flora Peter*

From *W. J. Thompson*

'HOME WORDS' SERIES. NO. 154.

GWHF15_449. A more religious Christmas postcard. Many sent postcards because the postage was cheaper than that for envelopes.

GWHF15_447. The many families who had suffered bereavement still felt the need to [send] Christmas Cards. This is a typical card sent by such a family: black ribbon and black [...]

GWHF15_451. A card from the front to family at home. 'We are on the Vistula beach, and fight for our country. What we could not achieve in 1914-15, 1916 will soon bring us.'

GWHF15_452. A comic Christmas card, making a joke of invasion and the best use for a German uniform.

GWHF15_450. A German Christmas postcard with a message felt by both sides: 'Glory to God in the highest, and peace to the people on earth.' The thre flags represent Germany, Austria and Bulgaria. Turkey, not being a Christia country, although an ally, is not included.

GWHF15_455. This card from the front must have been sent by the hundreds. As it was Christmas, the censor took no notice of the instructions.

Day by day chronology

January

1   Retail Food Price index (RFP) up 18% from start of war. Government starts to release skilled workers from the army.

2   In occupied Belgium, Cardinal Mercier is arrested for writing against German cruelty.

4   The Stock Exchange reopens but suspends traders and clerks who are of enemy origin if not naturalised.

6   Kitchener reviews war in House of Lords.

7   In France the sale of absinthe is prohibited.

8   Certain Turkish banks granted licences to continue trading in France, Egypt, Cyprus and conquered parts of the Ottoman Empire.

9   King and Queen visit Indian wounded at Brighton.

19 Zeppelin air raids on Yarmouth and King's Lynn – 4 killed and 16 injured. The Court of Appeal determines that, for business purposes, the test of a person being an enemy is their address or residence, not their nationality.

25 In Germany, government decree seizes all grain and flour stocks from 1 February.

February

1   Bread and flour rationing begins in Berlin and becomes national in June. Each person allowed just over four pounds a week. In Austria the metal shortage is addressed by formation of 'Metal Central Ltd' responsible for requisitioning all scrap metal. During the month the industrial truce ends, 209,000 days are lost by forty-seven strikes. Over 15% of workforce has enlisted. First all-women-run military hospital opens in Endell Street, London.

4   Germany declares waters round the United Kingdom a war region as from 18 February.

5   Commons votes an army of 3 million men with a further 32,000 for the navy.

6   Highest wheat prices for forty years. Demand by Commons for government control rejected.

7   Foreign Office justifies use of neutral flag to evade capture at sea.

11 Aeroplane raid on Colchester and Essex – no casualties.

12 Holland protests to Germany about U-boat blockade.

13 Railwaymen get the first war bonus in their pay. Turkish committee of Union & Progress decides to exterminate the Armenians.

16 Disabled Soldiers and Sailors Employment Committee formed.

18 King and Queen visit exchanged POWs from Germany.
20 Admiralty 'land ships' conference.
24 Austrian government takes over all grain and flour stocks.
25 King and Churchill inspect Royal Naval Division before it leaves for the Dardanelles.
26 Welsh Guards formed.
27 Second War loan in Germany.

March

1   RFP index now 24% above August 1914.
4   Admiralty decide that POW crew of U29 cannot receive honourable treatment. Reprisals threatened by Germany.
5   Issue of 3% Exchequer bonds announced.
7   London hit by flu epidemic.
8   Bill introduced to give government power over munitions works.
9   Thirty-four trades Trade Unions agree to expedite munitions output. Officers in uniform forbidden to visit nightclubs.
11 German treasury approves 2 million reichmarks to support Russian revolutionary propaganda.
16 *Customs (War Powers) Act* allows Customs and Excise officers to confiscate and condemn any goods suspected of being of enemy origin.
17 Women's War Service Register opened but by end of year is considerably short of target of 40,000.
19 Holland protests against Allied blockade.
20 Reichstag votes third War Credit against considerable opposition.
26 Dutch troops ordered to German border as invasion seems imminent. Local authorities in Germany authorised to ban the sale of alcohol, and production cut of 40 % malt in breweries.
28 First US citizen killed during sinking of British SS *Falaba* by U-boat.
29 Lloyd George tells nation that 'drink is more dangerous than Germany or Austria'. St. Dunstan's war blind hostel opens.
30 King offers total alcohol abstinence in Royal Household for the duration.
31 Home Secretary appoints a committee of enquiry into recruiting of men from the retail trades. Armaments Output Committee to organise skilled labour. In France absinthe is prohibited.

April

1   Scheme for a 'Dockers' Battalion' at Liverpool published. In Britain Union unemployment lowest for twenty-five years. Rosa Luxemburg imprisoned in Berlin for attacking the German Army.

5 King George prohibits use of alcoholic drinks in any of the royal households. John Redmond addresses the National Volunteer Convention at Dublin. Two German officer POWs escape from camp in Denbigh.

6 Government appoints committee on munitions.

7 Appeal by the churches for restraint in the use of alcohol.

8 In France the Class of 1916 is called up to make good losses so far. Armenian massacres begin 'for alleged cooperation with the Russians'.

11 Escaped German officers recaptured.

13 Munitions Committee meets under the chairmanship of Lloyd George.

14 Zeppelin raid on Tyneside by naval airship L9 which drops thirty-one incendiary bombs at Wallsend – two injured. In Belgium the Red Cross is suppressed.

15 Zeppelin raid on Essex and Suffolk by airships L5 and L6 – no casualties.

16 Aeroplane raid on Faversham, Sittingbourne and area – no casualties.

19 Further order to exterminate Armenians – about 55,000 murdered. Record day at London Central recruiting office.

20 Prime Minister denies British operations are hampered by a lack of munitions.

22 Passenger traffic between England and Holland suspended.

23 In Vienna, bread is of poor quality and flour hardly available. Pensions granted for dependants of civilians killed on War Department work.

26 Italy secretly joins the Allies. Asquith and Kitchener address Parliament on German war crimes.

29 Incendiary bomb raid on Suffolk by army airship LZ38 – three casualties. Lloyd George announces the government scheme with regard to alcoholic drinks - a drink tax.

30 In occupied Lille, bread ration cards introduced.

May

2 German notices in New York press warn that ships flying Allied flags in a war zone will become targets.

4 Budget estimated expenditure £1,6632,654,000 introduced; estimated revenue £270,332,000. Drink tax abandoned but duty increased.

5 Kaiser allows Zeppelins to attack docks and war factories in east London.

7 Zeppelin raid on Southend – 1 killed and 2 injured. Lusitania torpedoed off south west coast of Ireland. 1,198 men, women and children drowned, including 124 US citizens. Compulsory three-year bonding replaces increased liquor duties.

10 Anti-German demonstrations in London and Liverpool as a result of the sinking of the Lusitania.

11 Russian Red Cross flag day held in London.

12 Further anti-German riots.

13 British government decides to intern all enemy aliens of military age and strip enemy royalty of their British Honours.

14 Internment of enemy aliens begins.

16 Zeppelin raid on Ramsgate – 2 killed and 1 injured. King begins visits to factories, hospitals and shipyards in the north.

17 Lloyd George persuades Asquith to form coalition government. Kitchener asks for another 300,000 men. London tramway men lose strike for extra war bonus.

19 Age limit for recruits fixed at 40 and height requirement reduced to 5ft 2in.

21 Churchill dismissed.

22 A three-train collision in Scotland, the worst in British railway history, kills 226, including 214 men of 52 Division en route for Gallipoli.

23 National flag day in France to raise funds for the nine occupied departments.

25 Coalition Ministry formed with twelve Liberals and eight Tories. Nationalists approve the refusal of John Redmond to take office.

26 Zeppelin raid on Southend – 3 killed and 3 wounded. British Liquor Control Board formed.

30 First air raid on London when Zeppelins raid East London – 7 killed and 35 wounded.

June

1 RFP index now 32% up on August 1914. Food position in Vienna saved by Germans sending 2,000 wagons of flour. In Britain, first women skilled workers in private Glasgow munitions factory, the cotton industry allows female substitution and the National Union of Railwaymen accepts women members. To help munitions output in France, 100,000 conscripts diverted to munitions factories.

4 Zeppelin raid on Kent and Essex by L10 and on Hull by SL3 – 8 injured. Bill to create Ministry of Munitions introduced.

6 Zeppelin raid on Hull, Grimsby and the East Riding – 52 bombs killed 24 and injured 40. One Zeppelin destroyed by Lt. R Warneford, RN.

9 Ministry of Munitions Act passed.

15 Zeppelin raid on Northumberland and Durham – 18 killed and 72 injured. French bomb Karlsruhe factories causing 84 civilian casualties. Daily cost of the war now £2,666,000. Parliament votes £250 million credit for the war effort.

16 Lloyd George takes the oath as Minister of Munitions.

17 Armenian massacres continue. Food production committees formed in Britain.

18 Two Glasgow iron ore merchants jailed for trading with Krupps.

19 Tribich Lincoln, ex-MP for Darlington, committed for trial on charges of spying.

23 Carl Frederick Muller, a German spy, shot at the Tower of London. Prime Minister announces forthcoming bill on the registration and organisation of national resources.

24 Coalition government formed under Prime Minister Asquith. War Munition Volunteer Scheme begins.

27 In France, a national flag day raised money for orphans.

29 National Registration Bill introduced by Mr Walter Long. This required the registration of all people between the ages of 15 and 65 resident in England, Wales, Scotland, Scilly Isles and (with reservations) in Ireland. Exchanged wounded POWs arrive home. Prime Minister and Bonar Law give speeches at the Guildhall about the need to economize.

30 Welsh miners' dispute settled. Britain now has nearly $1 billion credit deficit with United States due to munitions purchases.

July

2 Ministry of Munitions formed and Munitions of War Act passed with 46,000 women workers enrolling in the first week. Munitions tribunals set up. In neutral America, a German Cornell University tutor plants a bomb which destroys Senate reception room. He also shot and wounded W. Pierpoint Morgan.

4 Aeroplane raid on East Suffolk – no casualties. The Tsingtao pilot, Sub-Lt. Pluschow and comrade escape from Donington Hall in Derbyshire. Pluschow escapes to Holland and then to Germany but partner is caught.

9 Kitchener appeals for more recruits in speech at Guildhall. By July there are 2million volunteers in camps across the country.

12 South Wales miners' conference rejects government proposals.

13 £570 million (besides £15 million through the Post Office) subscribed to War Loan. Strikes made an offence.

14 National Registration Bill passes the House of Lords.

15 Welsh miner's strike settled by Lloyd George. *National Registration Act* becomes law. German spy, Robert Rosenthal, hanged at Wandsworth prison.

17 Women's right-to-serve procession starts at the Victoria embankment, London, organised by Christabel and Emmeline Pankhurst and the Women's Social and Political Union.

19 Lady Moir and Lady Cowan establish scheme for training ladies to undertake weekend work to relieve women workers at the Vickers armaments factory, Erith, Kent. Government insurance against air and naval bombardment begins.

20 Welsh miners' strike settled.

21 Over 800,000 married recruits drawing separation allowance.

23 Italian planes bomb Innsbruck in Austria. A quarter of British doctors are serving with the forces.

25 Daily Mirror propaganda picture purporting to show German officers with gold and silver loot turns out to have been taken before the war.

27 Parliament informed of military losses so far: Royal Navy – 9,106; army – 330,995.

28 Debate on compulsory service. Germans bomb St. Omer and Nancy.

30 Haicke Janssen and Willem Roos, two German-Dutch spies, are shot at the Tower of London. French bomb Freiburg.

August

1   Through a Swiss intermediary, the British government trades rubber to Germany in return for binoculars. RFP index up 34% since August 1914.

3   Treasury appeals for public to use banknotes and not gold.

4   Anniversary service held at St. Paul's in London and in many other places across the country. Germans arrest Edith Cavell for helping Allied servicemen escape. Striking Belgian coalminers are fired on by German army. Official total of British military personnel killed is 75,957.

6   345 establishments declared 'controlled' under *Munitions of War Act*.

7   National Relief Fund stands at £5,431,671 in one year. France releases skilled workers back to industry.

9   Zeppelin raid on Goole, East Riding, Suffolk and Dover – 17 killed, injured. One raider destroyed at Dunkirk when returning to base.

12   Work on first tank started.

13   Three German naval officer POWs just fail to reach U38 off Llandudno after escaping from Dyffryn Aled Camp in north Wales.

14   Zeppelin raid on Essex and East Sussex – 6 killed and 24 injured.

15   National Registration of all males and females aged between 15 and 25 years. Austrians bomb Venice.

16   Cumberland coast bombarded from sea – no casualties.

17   Zeppelin raid on Kent, Essex and London – 10 killed and 48 injured.

18   Offices of the *Labour Leader* newspaper raided by the government.

21   Government declares cotton absolute contraband.

24   French bomb Mülheim.

25   French bomb Dillingen steelworks. 12,000 south Wales miners win war bonus strike.

26   Shipbuilding strike on Clydeside.

27   South Wales Miners' Federation refuse Mr Runciman's award. Government refuses to meet them in further conferences.

28   Germans bomb Compiègne.

31   South Wales coalfield dispute finally ended after considerable government concessions.

September

1   Sixteen national shell factories in production.

2   The King and Lord Kitchener inspect 2nd Canadian Division prior to its leaving for the front.

4   German citizens subscribe £601.5 million for 3rd War Loan.

6   French bomb Saarbrücken.

7   Zeppelin raid on East Suffolk and London - 18 killed and 38 injured. Unrest among railway

workers in South Wales. The majority of the British War Policy Committee want conscription.

8 Zeppelin raid on London, causing major fire in the City district, Norfolk and the North Riding – 26 killed and 94 injured.

9 Lloyd George stirs up Labour at TUC Congress 'With you victory is assured, without you our cause is lost…This country is not doing its best'. Ernst Melin, a German spy, is shot in the Tower of London.

11 Zeppelin raid on Essex – no casualties.

12 Zeppelin raid on Essex and East Suffolk – no casualties.

13 Aeroplane raid on Margate – 2 killed and 6 wounded. Zeppelin raid on East Suffolk – no casualties.

15 Vote of further credit brings total so far to £900 million for the year and £1,262,000,000 since the start of the war.

16 Taff Vale railway dispute ended.

17 Debate in House of Commons on National Service. Augusto Roggen shot as a spy in the Tower of London.

19 Fernando Buschman, a German spy, shot in the Tower of London.

21 Budget introduces new taxes; 50% on excess profits and on certain imports on grounds of foreign exchange and luxuries. Raised taxes – by 40% on income tax; postal charges; imports of certain comestibles, tobacco, motor-spirit, patent medicines. Exemption from income tax limited to £130; scale of abatements on larger incomes reduced. War now costing £4.5 million a day.

22 French bomb Stuttgart. Germans shoot four Lille citizens for helping French soldiers reach their lines and another for spying.

24 Liquor control regulations applied to the areas of Greater London.

30 Labour meeting resolves that the voluntary system with special recruiting campaign is sufficient and that there is no need for conscription.

October

1 RFP up 5%.

3 French bomb Metz.

5 Lord Derby made Director General of recruiting and calls on all fit men aged eighteen to forty-one to volunteer by 12 December.

7 Labour leaders appeal for volunteers for the army.

11 Lord Derby produces recruiting scheme; forty-six call up groups with married men being the last to be called-up. Treating prohibited.

12 Edith Cavell executed at Brussels.

13 Five-strong Zeppelin raid on Norfolk, Suffolk, the Home Counties and London - 71 killed and 128 injured.

15 State of war between Britain and Bulgaria from 10pm.
23 King George appeals for more men.
24 In neutral America, two German agents arrested and charged with conspiracy to destroy munitions ships leaving New York.
27 Food Home Production Committee urges more intense farming with guaranteed prices and the use of female labour.
28 'L2' circular, setting out women's wages for munitions workers.

November

1 King George returns to England after his accident in France on 28 October.
2 Asquith pledges to call up single men first and that conscription will only occur by general consent.
6 Suspension of *The Globe* for publishing misleading statements about Lord Kitchener.
8 Drastic criticism in the House of Lords of the government's measures, especially the press censorship. Enlistment of underground coal workers stopped.
10 German sabotage suspected as cause of great fire at Bethlehem Steel Company in South Bethlehem, Pennsylvania and in two other industrial accidents. Commons vote a further £400 million in war credit.
11 Lord Derby warns unmarried men of compulsion if they fail to enlist voluntarily before 30 November; marriage after Registration Day will not provide exemption from service. Asquith, Bonar Law, Lloyd George and McKenna form War Council. Churchill resigns from cabinet and joins BEF.
14 Austrian aircraft bomb Verona.
16 Manpower shortage means Italian government call-up Class of 1896.
17 New budget trebles beer duties.
25 First French Victory Loan raises £580 million. In Britain government restricts rents for the duration plus six months to pre-war levels.
26 Mr Stanton, Independent Labour candidate, stands as a protest against pacifist and anti-recruiting policy of late Keir Hardie, and wins the seat by 4,206 votes.
29 London licensing hours reduced to 5½ a day.
30 French call up Class of 1917.

December

1 RFP index now 44% up on August 1914 prices. Banks to close at 3pm instead of 4pm. Rail passengers ordered to pull down blinds at night. In Germany, butter is scarce and copper roofs in Berlin removed for armament use.

4   Henry Ford's peace ship *Oscar II* sails from America with peace women and journalists. The aim is to get the boys out of the trenches and home for Christmas.
6   Munitions Ministry controls 2,026 factories.
8   Hosiery and woodworking trades agree to pay women men's rates.
9   Suspected incendiary fires burn down Du Pont Company factory town in Virginia and 500,000 bushels of wheat for Allies in Pennsylvania.
11 Rush of recruits to volunteer during the last two days under the age group system.
12 Lord Derby's recruiting campaign closed.
16 New 5% Exchequer Bonds issued at par.
20 Groups of single men called up, as per the Derby Scheme.
25 The King sends Christmas message to his troops. In Glasgow, Lloyd George is shouted down by shop stewards during speech on the need for 80,000 skilled munitions workers.
28 Cabinet decides for compulsion – single men before married men. In Sweden, peace ship *Oscar II* found to have 4,000lb of rubber on board destined for Germany.
31 Unemployment at 1% is the lowest since 1872. Imports up 18% on 1914 and exports down 11%.

Bibliography, Sources and Further Reading

Baer, C. H. *Der Völkerkreig. Volumes 3 to10*. Julius Hoffmann. 1916.

Barnett, L.M, *British Food Policy during the First World War*. Allen & Unwin. 1985.

Becker, J. *The Great War and the French People*. Berg. 1990.

Bilton, D. *Hull in the Great War*. Pen & Sword. 2016.

Bilton, D. *Reading in the Great War*. Pen & Sword. 2016.

Bilton, D. *The Home Front in the Great War – Aspects of Conflict*. Leo Cooper. 2003.

Charman, I. *The Great War, The People's Story*. Random House. 2014.

Chickering, R. *Imperial Germany and the Great War, 1914-1918*. Cambridge University Press. 2005.

Fridenson, P. (Ed.) *The French Home Front. 1914-1918*. Berg. 1992.

Gregory, A. *The Last Great War. British Society and the First World War*. Cambridge University Press. 2008.

Hastings, M. *Catastrophe*. William Collins. 2013.

Herwig, H.H. *The First World War. Germany and Austria-Hungary 1914-1918*. Arnold. 1997.

Horn, P. *Rural Life in England in the First World War*. Gill and MacMillan. 1984.

http://www.theroyalscots.co.uk/page/the-quintinshill-gretna-train-crash-22-may-1915

Kennedy, R. *The Children's War*. Palgrave Macmillan. 2014.

Kocka, J. *Facing Total War. German Society 1914-1918*. Berg. 1984.

Markham, J. *Keep the Home Fires Burning*. Highgate Publications. 1988

Martin, C. *English Life in the First World War*. Wayland. 1974.

Marwick, A. *The Deluge. British Society and the First World War*. Macmillan. 1973.

Marwick, A. *Women at War*. Fontana. 1977.

Reetz, W. *Eine ganze welt gegen uns*. Ullstein. 1934.

Rex, H. *Der Weltkrieg in seiner Rauhen wirklichkeit*. Hermann Rutz. 1926.

Stein, W. *Um Vaterland und Freiheit Volumes 2 and 3*. Hermann Montanus. 1915.

The Berkshire Chronicle.

The Hull Times.

The Hull Daily Mail.

The Reading Standard.

Turner, E.S. *Dear Old Blighty*. Michael Joseph. 1980.

Unknown. *Großer Bilder Atlas des Weltkrieges. Volumes 1, 2, 3, 4, 5 & 20*. Bruckemann. 1915.

Unknown. *History of the War. Volumes 5 to 9*. The Times. 1915.

Unknown. *The Illustrated War News. Volumes 4 to 8*. Illustrated London News and Sketch, Ltd., 1914 & 1915.

Unknown. *Illustrated London News. January – December 1915*. Illustrated London News and Sketch Ltd., 1915.

Unknown. *Illustrierte Geschichte des Weltkrieges 14/19 Volume 3*. Union Deutsche Verlagsgesellschaft. 1919.

Unknown. *Kreigsalbum. Sonderheft der Woche No. 23 & 24*. August Scherl. 1915.

Unknown. *Kreigsalbum. Sonderheft der Woche No. 25*. August Scherl. 1916.

Unknown. *Kriegschronik August 1914 – July 1915*. Unknown. 1915.

Unknown. *Punch, Volume CXLVIII*. Punch. 1915.

Unknown. *Kamerad in Westen*. Societäts-verlag/Frankfurt am Main. 1930.

Various. *Thuringen im und nach dem Weltkrieg*. Lippold. 1920.

Williams, J. *The Home Fronts*. Constable & Co Ltd. 1972.

Winter, J. M. *The Experience of World War 1*. Equinox (Oxford) Ltd. 1986.

Winter, J. *The First World War. Volume III* Civil Society. Cambridge University Press. 2014.

Wilson, H.W. (Ed.) *The Great War. The Standard History of the All Europe Conflict. Volumes 4 & 5*. Amalgamated Press 1914 and 1915.

Index